JOHN WINTERS

Mental Toughness For Entrepreneurs

Copyright © 2019 by John Winters

All rights reserved. No part of this publication may be reproduced, stored or transmitted in any form or by any means, electronic, mechanical, photocopying, recording, scanning, or otherwise without written permission from the publisher. It is illegal to copy this book, post it to a website, or distribute it by any other means without permission.

John Winters has no responsibility for the persistence or accuracy of URLs for external or third-party Internet Websites referred to in this publication and does not guarantee that any content on such Websites is, or will remain, accurate or appropriate.

First edition

*This book was professionally typeset on Reedsy.
Find out more at reedsy.com*

Contents

SELF DISCIPLINE INTRODUCTION	1
Why Are You Doing This?	5
What Is Self-Discipline	15
Your Friendship With Pain	22
The Culture Of Cause and Effect	29
The Mind	33
The Body	58
Lifestyle And Nutrition	77
The Martial Way	86
Managing Ourselves	111
Finding Focus	118
The Secret Of Sacrifice	123
Mental Toughness	129
ENTREPRENEURSHIP INTRODUCTION	137
What is Entrepreneurship?	139
How To Become An Entrepreneur	144
Entrepreneurship Success	148
The Common Mistakes that First Time Entrepreneurs Must...	156
The 5 Skills Of A Good Entrepreneur	159
The Startup Business	175
Online Entrepreneurship	191
Social Media Marketing For Online Businesses	220
Lifestyle Design	236
Conclusion	248
Thank You	250

1

SELF DISCIPLINE INTRODUCTION

Here is the cold hard reality of a successful life. To live a life of meaning and significance you need self-discipline. You can't compromise on this. You can not achieve great success on this planet without a high level of Self-discipline.

There is a reason why professions where life and death are part of the job, depends on Self-Discipline. Jobs like the military, coastguard and others depend on the structure and stability needed to do their jobs efficiently and stay safe in a volatile world.

Normal Discipline usually gets maintained by some form of external threat or punishment from a commander or leader. This type of discipline is found at a lower level in a normal society with its laws. Where if you break the law you go to jail.

This form of discipline at a very high level is common in recruit training in the military. This is very effective in laying a foundation of discipline in a short amount of time. The military then achieves the long term goal that the soldier will leave basic training with some sense of Self Discipline. Within the unit, discipline will build trust and order. This will lead to efficiency, confidence, and control.

Self Discipline is a higher level of Discipline. Self Discipline is where external threats are no longer the motivating factor for the following of rules. The person applying Self-discipline becomes the authority over himself. He is now the master over his own life. This type of discipline can be traced back to all great warrior traditions like Samurai or Spartans that approached Self-Discipline as a way of life. Self Discipline was a code to achieve greater goals like Self Mastery. They knew Self Discipline leads to Self Mastery and that led to Control, power, and success.

Special Operations Units like the Green Berets and Navy Seals depends on Self Discipline. A lot of times the operators work alone or in small groups without any supervision. They are independent soldiers. That is why they get referred to as operators. The operators don't have an external threat of maintaining discipline. They get trained to become Self-disciplined. They get taught the value of Self-Discipline and they know that Self-Discipline is one thing they can always depend on. It's the one thing that will make the difference between success and failure.

These men succeed because they live by a code. The foundation of this code is Self Discipline. Self Discipline allows them to operate in extreme conditions and be successful consistently. This Self Disciplined code allows operators to be unaffected by external factors like death, danger, chaos, uncertainty and human coercion.

In today's world Self Discipline is very rare. The modern human mind has become very weak and fragile. The majority of people have lost control of their minds. They just go with the flow and have no mental toughness. They live with the mindset of the victim and has given away their personal sovereignty by not having any form of Self-Discipline.

You can just go on social media for 10 minutes to see the low level of physical and mental Self-Discipline. You see people complaining about being overweight and doing nothing about it. Or people being depressed and unhappy and not taking control of the situation. People having no money but spending the money they do have on garbage. People reacting angrily and wasting hours on social media arguing with strangers because they don't have the Self-Discipline to control their emotions.

In today's world, we live in a strange environment where discipline and Self Discipline is seen as this alien thing. It's this thing that soldiers, athletes, and other professionals do but it's not something a normal person does. People buy into this culture of mediocrity and then wonder why they don't achieve anything of great value.

Self Discipline can be taught but it can't be forced like normal discipline. Self-Discipline can be encouraged. That encouragement I will try and give you in this book. I will share with you this fundamental truth. You are ultimately in charge of your life. You are responsible for all your actions. Everything that happened to you is your responsibility. By adopting Self Discipline and building a code of Self Discipline you can take control of your life. With this control will come a great amount of power. With this power, you can create any amount of success you want. However, you have to make a choice. A choice to start living by a code of Self Discipline or going back to mediocrity and driving into the shadows.

Just a warning before you start this book. This book is for people who want to be successful in life. This is the book is for people who want to go after life with everything they have. This book is for people who want to not just be successful in one area of life but be successful in all areas of life. If you are just looking for a book that makes you feel a bit better then stop reading now. If you are just looking for a book that will tell you how many push-ups to do and go on a diet then stop now.

This book will dive into the heart and soul of Self-discipline so that you can be successful in life. More importantly, it's about creating a culture of Self Discipline, It's not just something you try out for a while and then go back to what you were doing. It's a way of life.It's part of who you are.Or its part of who you are becoming.

If you are ready to start transforming your life then keep on reading.I think you already made your choice since you are reading this book. So let's get started.

2

Why Are You Doing This?

Why do you need self-discipline? Why are you reading this book? What made you study self-discipline? I get it! You want to get up earlier, go to the gym and all those little things that are all very important. But what is your real "why"?

Why are you doing this? The reason I ask this is that if you're "why" is not big enough then the rest of this book is not going to help you.

I see this a lot. Guys get a glimpse of motivation and they want to change.
   Or its new years again and everyone is making resolutions. So you get fired up and you start making all these promises to yourself.

You tell yourself I'm going to lose weight, I'm going to get my money right, I'm going to start eating healthy, I'm going to spend less time online.

These things are great. So you make your new years resolutions and you get fired up. You start firing the first few weeks but gradually you lose steam. All that motivation you had just 2 or 3 weeks ago is gone.

So tell yourself "Good effort but this discipline thing is maybe just not for me."

The Resistance

Here is the reality of building self-discipline. Before you start you need to go look at your why. Why are you really doing this? Those reasons I mentioned above like losing weight is cute and all but that's not going to get you to fully committed to what you want.

Because guess what?As soon as you start to change all kinds of funny stuff will happen. You will see friends beginning to question you about why you are doing this. They will tell you things like "I like the old you better".They will tell you "You are acting kind of weird" or "Come out drinking with us".They will fire all these things at you and test your resolve.

Most people, unfortunately, fold right here and throw in the towel. They break at the first resistance. Friends and acquaintances are just one form of resistance you will come across. There are many forms of resistance. The most dangerous form of resistance is internal resistance

What is The Internal Resistance?

The author Steven Pressfield of the great book 'The War Of Art' gave it a name he called it the "resistance".The resistance is that voice that comes up when you want to start making moves in your life. It's the voice that comes up when you want to go running. The voice will whisper in your ear for example, "You don't need to go run now, its cold outside, let's do it tomorrow. "

Or the voice will say "Go buy that pizza it looks great. Who needs these healthy meals you eat every night?" The voice of the resistance will be a constant pain in the ass. It will always try and stop you when you have important things to do.

Your "Why" Needs To Be Strong

Family, friends the resistance and other factors trying to stop you is a reality. The reason most people stop is that they have a weak "why?".You need to go ask yourself why are you doing this? Why are you really doing this? There has to be something deeper driving you. Only you can answer this question.

Marketing secrets

In marketing, they have figured out that humans get motivated usually by 2 very powerful forces. The forces of pain and pleasure. Pain and pleasure by itself are just 2 things we experience on a daily basis. However, it can be incredibly powerful tools if you use them effectively.

In this book about self-discipline, we need something to make our "why" incredibly powerful. A great way to find your "why" is to go to the two powerful tools of pain and pleasure.

For example, why do you want to lose weight? To look good? Feel better? Whatever your reason is there has to be something more profound. Let's take pain as an example.

When you are fat you might see people pointing at you and laughing because you look fat in your t-shirt. How do you feel about that? Does it feel nice to be embarrassed? No, of course not. It causes pain right? It feels bad.

If this happens all the time the pain gets more and more intensive and severe.Instead of running from this pain how about using it to get what you want?How about remembering very clearly how that pain felt and telling yourself you never want to feel like that ever again.

So whenever you find yourself in a situation where you want to quit than take a moment and think about the pain. Feel that pain deeply and then just get up and do it because the pain will drive you to get there.

For me, the pain was related to money. For a time in my life, I experienced so much pain with money that I would do anything to not experience that feeling of pain related to money. That pain became me "why". Ask yourself how much pain you will feel if you don't do that thing that you're supposed to do? Then realize you never want to experience that again.

Pleasure has a similar power although I find pain to be working better for me. If you want to do something for example not eat the cake then ask yourself this. How much pleasure will you have when you take your shirt off, and you look like an absolute boss walking around? Imagine the pleasure of the compliments and the admiring looks from friends and strangers. Imagine the respect you will get for being so dedicated to creating a body like that. These images in your mind of pleasure should be strong enough for you to get going. These feelings of pleasure will be your "why".

You Must Be Willing To Do Things You Have Never Done Before

After you figured out your "why" we need to get to a very important reality. This reality will make or break your attempt to become self-disciplined. Self-Discipline is a tool to live a powerful life. But its also a tool to live a very successful life and achieve your goals.

For you to get what you want in life you need self-discipline. However you will not succeed with self-discipline if you don't accept this important reality. The reality is this: You must be willing to do things that you have never done before. If you don't you will not be successful.

You are going to have to do many things you don't like. Therefore you will have to do things you have never done before. So you will be uncomfortable and you will constantly feel like you want to give up.

You Must Become The Ruler Of Your Own World

Most People on this planet are in an unconscious state of chaos. The world in its natural state is in chaos. When humans created civilization they formed a stable environment and brought some form of structure to the random chaos on planet earth. However on individual level chaos still exists for most.

Most people allow external forces and their own mind and emotions to control and dominate them. They are not the masters of their own world. For you to get control of your own world you need to adapt Self-Discipline. If you are successful with this you will take control back. You will then find that you have a new reality that is built upon power. This power will be new for you. You will experience true freedom for this first time. Freedom from random events and impulses.Freedom from opinions, people and circumstances. For the first time, you will be the master of your world. You will be free.

Take Ownership

You have to take ownership of everything in your life. If you shift responsibility for what happens in your life to others you will keep on losing. When you are not responsible for what happens in your life then it means you are a victim. Victims are not in control of their own lives. When you take ownership of everything you will take power back in your life.

Going After An Ideal

We live in a world where 99% of the time limitations will be pointed out to you in the first ten seconds of a conversation. Let's look at two scenarios. I know you know the conversation in Scenario A. It goes something like this. "I have an idea to start a new company". Your friend looks at you and says something like, "Yea but what if you don't make it or where will you get the money?" This conversation is an example of the most common mindset we live in today.

Let's look the at scenario B, but it's one that you will probably never hear in your average day. "I have an idea to start a company", your friend replies, "Well that is an awesome idea. Call me if I can help you with anything. I know you're going to be successful."

You have two scenarios; unfortunately, scenario one is the reality in which the majority of people on the planet live in. It's a cynical world where people don't like it if you go after something you feel passionate about or become highly successful in something you actually care about.

This is just one example of this mindset. It's not just something we see in our work life. It has crept into all areas of society. You can look at any area of your life. I bet you won't remember the last time someone totally supported you in the actions you take.

I remember telling one my friends that I was planning to start a business. After I told him what I was planning, he reacted by saying, "Is that all?" Sure, I get it we need a reality check sometimes, but he could have said a thousand different things, however, he chose to be cynical in his first reaction. This is, unfortunately, the way many people react if you start going after things. If you do nothing and stay where you are, they are more comfortable. Then they will say nothing.

As soon as you go after something unusual or something that changes the status quo you will get resistance. If you quit your job and go after an entirely new career, you will get resistance. If you leave your church or religion, there will be resistance. If you move to another country there will be resistance, if you say you are turning pro there will be resistance, if you say you are going to be a doctor, there will be resistance.

Accept This As The Reality

Step one in changing your reality is to accept this as the reality of the majority of people out there. However, you have a choice. The choice is to get out of the Matrix (negative reality) and go after an ideal.

We have to go after an ideal. What does your ideal life look like? What is the perfect version of whatever you want to be? Think about your dream life and then go after it. It is our responsibility to step up and build a successful life. That is why we are here. If you want to elevate yourself above the masses of followers, then you have to go after an ideal.

What is the alternative? The alternative is going after a piece of crap that makes you miserable. And guess what? If you fail in the thing you love, you will be better for it. But if you go after a life you hate and you fail you will be miserable. Then you will look back at your life with regret.

Staying in your comfort zone and not going after an ideal means conforming to a mediocrity that is breaking the souls of men around the world.

You have to create your own sense of belonging by going after your ideal life. As long as that ideal is ethical and of service to your fellow humans. Don't go after something stupid, unethical or illegal that will hurt other people. That is not going after an ideal; it's going after stupidity.

So how do we go after the ideal?

Creating the best version of ourselves

As men, it's our duty to create the best versions of ourselves. By doing this, we serve not just ourselves but also our girlfriends, wives, partners, families, and society.

We can only be of service to the world when we go after our ideal. And this ideal is creating the best version of ourselves.

When I talk about creating the best version of ourselves, I don't mean being a little angel and acting perfectly all the time. We will still make mistakes and screw up. That's part of being a man.

By being the best version of ourselves means the following:

(1) Finding your purpose- why are you here?

Finding your purpose has many benefits, but one important benefit is that it might lead you to live a longer life. A recent study at Carleton University in Canada found some interesting results.

The results were published in Psychological Science, a journal of the Association for Psychological Science and it stated the following:

"Greater purpose in life consistently predicted lower mortality risk across the lifespan, showing the same benefit for younger, middle-aged, and older participants across the follow-up period."

(2)After you got your purpose figured out, sit down make a plan on how you are going to go after your purpose

(3)Step 3 is to go after this ideal you created with everything you have and not let anything or anyone get you off that purpose

(4) Don't be realistic.I'm not saying do something stupid, but what you are dreaming might seem crazy or unrealistic to other people, but don't let that stop you.

I know about a lot of people who were "unrealistic."Henry Ford, The Wright Brothers, Thomas Edison, Steve Jobs, and many others. These guys decided they are going all in on life.

This type of independent thinking will be hard to cultivate, and you will meet a lot of resistance. But independent thinking is super important for creating the best version of yourself. We have to walk alone if we want to go live a life that is above the mediocre. People will go after you and criticize you when you put yourself out there, but that is part of the climb.

<u>Superhero</u>

Joe Rogan always talks about the idea of being "the hero in your own movie".With that in mind ask yourself what will your hero do in this situation? Joseph Campbell also refers to similar ideas of heroes and ideals in his work. These types of archetypes are very powerful in keeping us motivated and moving us forward. In modern culture, we have forgotten to look at our past to find strength.

Warriors are not just people in the military or law enforcement. We are all warriors in a spiritual sense. We have to fight daily battles in our lives. At work in the boardroom, office and all other areas of life.

Creating a superhero version of yourself might sound weird, but it's a great way to start getting momentum. Going after this superhero ideal will elevate your life to the next level. In Asian cultures, this has been used for a very long time by warrior traditions to build confidence and strength.

(5)Dream big because what is the alternative?

If we don't dream big then what else do we have? Do we just settle? Do we just go for the socially acceptable or mediocre? No!! We have a responsibility to go after what we want. Because when you are 80 years old, you will have to look yourself in the mirror and admit that you did not go for it.

3

What Is Self-Discipline

Let's start at the dictionary definition of Self Discipline:

"The ability to control one's feelings and overcome one's weaknesses; the ability to pursue what one thinks is right despite temptations to give up and stop."

This, in a nutshell, is Self-Discipline. However, the attainment of self-discipline is challenging. Most people live without any form of discipline and the price they pay for that is unknown to them. They prefer not the pay the price of Self Discipline to live a successful and fulfilling life. Like they say "Ignorance is bliss".

Like I mentioned in the introduction of this book Self Discipline is slightly different from normal discipline. Normal discipline in the conventional military or rules in society has one thing in common. It has the threat of external force or punishment. However, Self-discipline is different.

Self Discipline is where external threats are no longer the motivating factor for following rules. The person applying Self-discipline becomes the authority over himself. He has made the choice to take control over his own life and ultimately his destiny. This is why elite special operations soldiers and elite athletes use Self-Discipline. They know the immense power they get through self-discipline.

Self Control

In order for you to become Self-Disciplined, you need to cultivate the ability to do the right thing on the right time whether you feel like or not. Your biggest obstacle to this goal will be Instant gratification.

Instant Gratification

Instant gratification is something that plagues the majority of people on this planet. We are all guilty of it sometimes, however Self-Disciplined individuals very rarely break their code and give in to the temptation.

What is Instant Gratification?

Instant gratification is the desire to experience pleasure right now and without any delay. You want something right now and that is it. Examples of instant gratification are parties, gossip, shopping, alcohol, drugs, smoking, sugar, fast food, social media likes and comments etc.

Delaying Gratification

Delaying gratification is the opposite. When you delay gratification, you have long term goals. You think long term to reach your objectives. You act accordingly and don't compromise to achieve your goals. You reject instant gratification for something much bigger. Your success is your only focus.

The key to all Self Discipline is delaying gratification. That means fighting all your natural impulses. Your brain is designed to keep you comfortable and help you survive. It does not care for your happiness. It has no regard for your goals and your self-discipline comes in the way of its impulse to get what it wants right now.

The Triune Brain Theory

The neuroscientist Paul D. MacLean created the Triune Brain Theory. In this theory, Maclean states that the human brain is actually 3 brains in one, hence the name "triune brain."

Let's take a look at the 3 brains MacLean refers to:

(1) The Reptilian brain

This is the oldest and most ancient part of the human brain. This part is very similar to the brains of lizards. This part of the brain has primitive processes like feeding, sex, exploration, dominance, and aggression. You will find this part of the brain at the brainstem and the cerebellum.

(2) Mammalian brain

MacLean states that after a very very long time a second brain evolved called the mammalian brain. This brain evolved over the first one and is today referred to as the limbic system.

"The old-mammalian brain, or the limbic system, adds behavioral and psychological resolution to all of the emotions and specifically mediates the social emotions such as separation distress/social bonding, playfulness, and maternal nurturance." (Jaak Panksepp in Affective Neuroscience: The Foundations of Human and Animal Emotions (1998).

The limbic system according to the scientist Panksepp also controls "subjective feelings and emotional responses."

Modern business and especially tech business has exploited the limbic system for massive profits. Think about all the social media platforms out there today. They are designed to exploit and reflect all the dominant human emotions.

Recently the entrepreneur and tech genius Elon Musk went on the Joe Rogan podcast. On the show, he said that the most successful social media platforms are the ones that resonate most with our Mammalian brain(limbic system)He goes on to say that these social media systems, represent an increasing share of society's total intelligence. Musk ended the topic saying this: "Imagine all those things, the sort of primal drives, there's all the things that we like and hate and fear, they're all there on the internet. They're a projection of our limbic system."

This is the reason why people get addicted to social media. People waste hours and hours of their lives on these platforms. They feel like they have no control over it.

(3)Neomammalian brain (Human Brain)

The Neomammalian brain or the human brain is the last part of the brain to develop. To put in simple terms the Neomammalian brain has to do with our logical and reasoning abilities. This is a uniquely human ability.

Humans Are Not Rational Most Of The Time

There is a perception with a lot of people that humans are very logical. Yes, we have moments of logic, but 90% of what we do is coming from the more ancient part of our brain and is anything but logical. We get dominated by the older and more primitive parts of the brain. This is the reason why it seems there is always a lot of chaos around the world. That is because there is. Sure we have made a lot of progress along the way, but we still struggle to keep it all together.

Conflict

We are in conflict with ourselves. Mainly because we are unaware of the massive power our brains have over our actions. Also, we do not know that we can do something about it and create better lives for ourselves. So this brain of ours is complex, and we need to keep an eye on it.

The problem with so many people letting their minds run free is that we now have so many social problems. These issues traced back to people just being out of the touch with the reality of their own minds. Another way of looking at it is like the movie The Matrix where people are stuck in an artificial reality, and they are not aware of it.

The people who are stuck in the matrix are the people who are the followers in society. They don't question anything and have lost the ability to think critically. They are under total control of their minds. They have no mental self-discipline.

Most modern societies have created a culture where we have lost touch with who we really are. In the western world especially people have started to evaluate human problems as these little things in crystal boxes that we need to medicate, assess and label as modern human problems.This process of modern human culture is the problem.We have started to evaluate ourselves as these supposedly rational beings that do things just because of the situation we are in. We have totally forgotten about the animal inside ourselves. We are not like monkeys, we are monkeys. We are a very advanced specie of primate that has a very complex brain. This brain and body has very ancient parts that humans tend to forget when we talk about problems in our lives or in society.

This Is The Challenge Of Self Discipline

The Reason I gave this particular description of the 3 brain theory is to give you and an understanding of the ancient forces you are struggling against. This is the reason why success is so hard. It's hard to consistently fight these very powerful forces. And if someone does not implement Self Discipline into their lives then success will stay a dream only. Self Discipline needs to be something that is a way of life.

Delaying Gratification is one of the biggest challenges for us. Instant gratification plagues most people on this planet. Most people want to get what they want right now. They want it now, and they want it without any concern for the long-term consequences. They allow those ancient parts of their brains like the limbic system to dominate them.

There is a constant battle going on every day of your life. This battle is doing what is right vs. what is nice, easy, fun and pleasurable.

Biology Is Ruthless

Earlier in this chapter, I gave a general explanation of the 3 brain theory and how complex human biology is. One thing that humans don't contemplate a lot is how ruthless biology as a whole is. This planet is one giant organism. Humans live here with other animals and plants. As a whole, we make up this giant melting pot of life. Earth itself is part of the universe. We are influenced by the sun, moon and everything else around us. We as humans have a very limited understanding of how things really work.

My point with all this is that you should always keep in mind how ruthless and brutal biology is. Like I mentioned before your goals, feelings, success, and life means nothing to it. Biology just steams forward like a machine. It's your responsibility to resist the forces that create havoc on your mind and body.

How Do We Resist It?

To resist our own biology and the biology of this planet we need to embrace self-discipline and take control of our natural impulses. But there is another key component that might seem unrelated to Self-Discipline. You need to constantly be learning. You should be reading books about human psychology, biology, and evolution, I get it you can't read everything but study the basics so you understand yourself and the world you live in better. This will give you a great insight into how Self-Discipline keeps everything together. You have to develop as a human.

Fighting That Voice(Impulses)

We live in magnificent ancient bodies. These bodies have brains that react to impulses. If you want to become Self Disciplined you need to recognize these impulses and resist them.

The payoff you will get for building Self Discipline is massive. If you do this right your life will change.

4

Your Friendship With Pain

Pain will be something you will have to confront. Most humans run when they are confronted by pain. Whenever you take positive actions like going to the gym, quit smoking, writing that report, eating healthy or getting up early, you might feel pain. You will feel discomfort. Your first thought will be to stop. This is where most people end their effort with Self-Discipline.

They start feeling discomfort and they give up. They feel pain the first time and immediately stop. They want to go back to comfort now. Instant gratification is what they want. They can't take the pain a bit longer to get the results they want. So they give up and run to comfort.

These shadows in our minds are scary for most humans. When they go into these territories in their minds for the first time they resist it, they turn around and run.

What you need to do is turn around and confront the pain. Make friends with it. When you start feeling discomfort smile at it and own it. Tell yourself that its fine to feel pain or discomfort. Once you feel the pain realize that this is your signal that you are doing the right thing. Walk through the darkness. Start loving these experiences because you know they are making you stronger.

People Don't Like Change

The obvious thing about self-discipline is that you need to change. But there is another thing that plagues humans. This is the fact that Humans hate change.

Most people will never change. Especially in today's comfortable environment where people get anything they want with the press of a button. They get seduced by modern comfort. So they delay change and improvement.

That is why things like new years resolutions never work. People are too comfortable and they want the instant gratification. So most people never change. But like I mentioned in the previous chapter biology is ruthless. Life goes on and before you know it all kinds of chaos has broken out.

For example, a person starts to get overweight and thinks about losing some weight by starting a new workout plan. So the person tells himself he will start in 3 weeks when the new year starts. So the new year starts and nothing happens. He thought about change for a few minutes but then got seduced by comfort and that doughnut on the table. He didn't listen to his friend who told him to be disciplined and start exercising and eating healthy.

So what happens? Biology strikes hard and ruthlessly. A year later he becomes seriously ill and the doctor says he is a diabetic. Something he could have prevented if he had self-discipline and took control of his life.

So yes biology waits for nobody. But in today's environment, there is another enemy that is allowed to seduce and comfort the masses of people out there. This enemy is feelings. The modern world is addicted to feelings.

They have given feelings absolute priority over everything else. If someone feels sad, angry, depressed and bad then the world has to stop and comfort that person. The world has been seduced by this addiction to feelings.

They have traded truth for comfort. They won't point out problems they will hide behind feelings. When a person can't walk up the stairs they will not say you are fat. They will say, "He is just a little tired".

When a person failed his test they won't say "You are lazy", they will say "He had a bad day".

When someone is late they won't point out the bad manners they will just say "That's ok".

We hide from the truth so we can feel comfy and coddled. In most developed countries like the US, Canada, and Europe people live in coddled spoilt societies. The results of this are that society as a whole is becoming weaker and weaker. Today's society gives each other hugs for everything. But unfortunately what many people need is slap in the face to wake up from the trance they are in.

This leads to people really struggling on an individual level to change when they have to. This also makes people give up very easily when they decide they want to change. They are mentally weak.

We mentioned the importance of accepting pain earlier in this chapter. The problem is that in today's world pain is avoided at all costs. The brutal reality of biology is that the clock is ticking and your time is running out. Every second you allow yourself to get seduced by emotion, warm hugs, participation trophies and modern comforts you are getting deeper into trouble.

Here is another newsflash. If you don't make the changes necessary to live your best life you will probably live a life of depression, unhappiness, and stress. This is just how biology rips comfort to pieces. Again, biology has no feelings whatsoever and if you don't get on the same playing field by adapting Self-Discipline you will lose. And lose badly.

Let me use an analogy to explain how it goes in life for most people. Let's imagine every person on this planet is on a ship on the ocean. This ship represents your life. This ship is made up of your life story. This ship includes everything. The way you live, what you eat, your lifestyle and self-discipline or the lack of self-discipline.

Now let's imagine everyone wants to go North because North is where success is. The problem is that most people that have no Self-Discipline in their lives think they are going North but they are actually heading South. South is where the rocks are. The rocks mean danger and death. Most people end up on the rocks.

So what happens when people hit the rocks? They freak out and act surprised. They don't know what happened. They don't understand how everything around them turned into chaos. Then they start remembering the new year's resolutions they didn't follow through on. They remember the time spent partying when they should have been studying. They remember all those doughnuts and ice cream they ate when should have been eating healthy. But now its too late.

Don't be one of those people who is going in the wrong direction. You need to realize the seriousness of the situation and make the changes necessary so you can go North.

What To Do If You Are On The Rocks Now?

If you are on the rocks now then I have some good news and some bad news. The good news is that you can still make it north. The bad news is you will have to not only accept pain as a friend, but you will also have to make it your brother. You will need to look for the pain. You will need to embrace pain so that you become so strong that the natural momentum of your efforts pushes you north.

The Bottom Line Of Self Discipline

You need to learn to do things you hate. The world we live in today tells us to just be comfortable and that we should avoid things we don't like. This is the biggest reason why so many people don't get what they want in life. To get what you want you to need to accept the following point: You have to start doing things you don't like doing. In fact, you need to become excellent at those things that you don't like doing.

A lot of people walk around saying that "I just want to follow my heart or my passion".Listen, that whole idea was built in a dream world. In reality, even the people that do things they love for a living sometimes have to do things they hate.

Talk to the most successful people on the planet and they will tell you the same thing. Sure I agree, find the thing you love, but to get there you might have to walk through a lot of crap. And guess what? Once you achieve the thing you want you still need to do some things you hate. This is the real world.

A lot of people quit their jobs and start their own businesses and then get a rude awakening. They thought now that they work for themselves they only get to do things they love. Unfortunately, the world of business doesn't work that way. Anything of value on this planet takes discipline and hard work to turn into reality.

This way of thinking is unfortunately widespread in the world we live in. Its especially prevalent in the online world of business and social media. The internet has created a massive opportunity for many people to create a living online and this has created the false idea of overnight success.

The whole modern entertainment industry including social media and others has created the false reality of overnight success. People buy into this idea of becoming rich and famous overnight. They see the post on social media showing someone posing in a car full of cash. The guy in the car says he became rich in a month and you can do the same. People buy into this rubbish.

Unfortunately, we now have a culture of entitlement. People want all their dreams to come true right now. They don't want to hear about things like hard work, perseverance. patience and self-discipline. They want the magic pill, the quick fix so that they can get that warm fussy feeling inside. The last thing they want is to do things they hate to get what they want. All they want is the big check and the pictures on social media.

You see it everywhere. In business, people start online and the first thing they ask is how they can outsource most of the work. I have nothing against delegating and outsourcing. However, that should not be your first priority. In fact, you need to do the hard work yourself first to get a better understanding of how your business works and what your employees go through. You need to do the hard work first before you earn the right to start playing the big boss man.

In fitness, people see their favorite movie star on TV and they think I want to look like that guy. The first thing they start looking for is some kind of supplement or protein powder that will build them that physique. They don't start with a workout and start doing the hard work necessary to get that body. In my own life, I hate running but I still do it because it gets me where I want to go in terms of my fitness and health goals. The upside of running totally outweighs the downside of my feelings towards running.

With dating and relationships, it's the same. A guy sees a beautiful woman somewhere and he asks his coworker to go ask the girl for her phone number. He doesn't have the courage to get into the "uncomfortable" situation and go talk to the girl. He wants all the upside with no downside.

Self-Discipline will teach you how to shut out all these voices in your head trying to stop you from success. Your discipline will keep you in check when you don't want to do the hard work necessary to get to where you want to go. Its now up to you to do the hard work to build a culture of Self Discipline in your life.

5

The Culture Of Cause and Effect

Talking about self-discipline is the easy part. Implementing Self-Discipline is the hardest part. Many people think that the daily actions of Self- Discipline are the hardest part. That is not the case. Although daily Self-Discipline is challenging its not the hard part. Implementing and building a culture of discipline in your life is the hard part. Creating rules for your life with a foundation of Self-Discipline is the hard part.

Once you have achieved the foundation and start living your code then Self-Discipline becomes a lot easier. Self-discipline structure will give you security and confidence. You will learn that once you become a Self-Disciplined individual that living by this code will become very important to you. It will become your new normal and something you will learn to take pride in.

Developing Self Discipline

You can't just have discipline in one area of life. It doesn't work that way and it's not effective. Slack off in one area and it influences all other areas of life.

Foundations

Cause and Effect

Before we start this chapter I want to make one point abundantly clear. The whole universe functions on a very important principle. This principle is called cause and effect. This means everything you do has an effect. Every action you take will lead to something else. Whether that something else is positive or negative is up to you. It's up to the choices you make every day. The sum total of those choices will lead to either success or failure in whatever you are doing in life. Everything you do matters.

The Culture of Self Discipline

The biggest mistake people make is dabbling in Self-Discipline. They think just doing one thing differently will get them what they want. They think they want Self-Discipline so they make a change in one area of their lives and think that is going to get them what they want. For example, they want to lose weight and think by just eating well and exercising they will reach their goals.

People think they want to try out self-discipline. So they think "I'm going to give it a week and see if it works" or "Let's try it for a month".They put one foot in the water but don't commit. Here is the reality: If you dont jump in the water and submerge yourself in a culture of Self -Discipline then you have already lost. You are done. Most people fail because they dabble in Self-Discipline. But there is a more important thing that they miss. The thing they don't do that make all the difference is that they don't make a commitment.

You Need To Make a Commitment

I see this all the time with guys who want to improve their lives. They want to get better but they hold back. They don't commit. They think if they "give it a go" they can tell everyone they gave it their best shot and it didn't work out. They think just trying will get them there.

There is a famous story of a Karate Master in Japan. In the story the master sees a student struggling to execute a move in class. The Master asked him what the problem is. The student answers and says, "I'm trying". The master looks at him and says, "Stop trying, just do it". This is the mindset most people have. They are "just trying" and at a subconscious level, they believe they can't do it. This subconscious belief holds them back from success. So they keep on "trying" and never just step up and do it.

Most people have a mental block or a disadvantage before they even begin. They have already decided they are lost. They have already decided on an unconscious level they can't do it. So they go in with a halfhearted effort so they can tell people and themselves that they "tried".

In the modern world, we lost this little thing called "faith" or "belief". You need to have faith in yourself that you will not just try Self Discipline but you will do it. Believe it and make a commitment to building a culture of Self Discipline and with that a culture of success. But you have to make a decision that that is the way that it's going to be.

Many people will hear me saying this and say "Ahh good talk but it's not that easy". Well yes, it's not easy, but nothing of any value is easy to get. Change the way you think about this and change your life. Make a decision today that you will become successful no matter what it takes. Self-Discipline will be the vehicle to get you there.

Everything in your life needs to change to make a massive transformation. If you want big results commit and go all in. If you want to get what you have never had before then you need to do what you have never done before.

6

The Mind

(1)The Mind

The mind is complex and is a place that creates your reality. The mind like mentioned earlier in this book is influenced by ancient and newer parts of the brain.

Emotions

Another major factor is emotions. Emotions are some of the most powerful forces in the universe. If you allow your emotions to get control of you then you will struggle to have a successful life. If you learn how to get control of your emotions you will feel that you gain more confidence and power in your life.

We live in a world addicted to emotions. People allow emotional addiction to dictate their choices and control their lives. You can just spend a few minutes on social media to see that. Better yet put on the news for a few minutes and you will see the emotional addiction everywhere.

The puppet masters of big corporations and governments have known for a long time that emotions have the power to control societies. They know that by creating certain emotions in society they can reach certain objectives. They also know most people will blindly follow their emotions without question. This is why people will spend hours arguing on social media comments. They let their anger take control of them and then waste hours arguing with a stranger they never met before.

The reality is that its natural to feel emotions. However, the question is how do you react to them?

There are ways to manage your emotions, for example, breathing techniques. The special operations forces are masters at getting control over emotions. Their lives are lived in a pressure cooker environment. If they don't learn to effectively manage their emotions they can lose their lives.

The problem for soldiers is not just the short term threat of death but also long term bad effects. The negative effects are things like depression, anxiety, trouble sleeping, irritability, heavy drinking or other symptoms of mental and physical stress.

Let's take a look at some ways you can manage your mind and emotions more effectively:

Breathing

Breathing can be a powerful tool to instantly get control over emotions like fear and anxiety. It's a very powerful technique that special operations units use and is called box breathing. Box breathing is a technique that uses a deep breath to calm down the heart rate and focus the mind.

It works like this:

-Start by trying to get into a relaxing position.Sit down if possible. If you can't sit then just stand where you are and close your eyes.

-Sit up straight and focus.

-Breath out to clear your lungs. You want to get rid of all the oxygen in your lungs

-Start by inhaling deeply and slowly through your nose. Do this slowly to the count of four.

-Focus now on holding this breath for another quiet count of four.

-Exhale through your mouth. Again this happens to the quiet slow count of four.

-Then wait for a slow count of four and repeat.

-You can do this exercise for a few minutes until you start feeling relaxed.

Meditation

If I can take one tool with me to a new reality, it would be meditation. Meditation is a superpower that is available to all of us for free. All you have to do is practice it and make it a habit. Sounds easy right?Well yes and no. If you can get yourself to do it, it becomes easy. The benefits are endless, and the quality of your life will improve.

There are many different opinions about meditation. Many people think that meditation is only done by monks. They also think that it's connected to only Buddhism or Hinduism. The truth is that meditation is open to anybody to use as a tool for self-improvement. It can be a secular or religious experience. You can give it whatever meaning you want, does not matter. The benefits you get will still be the same.

There are many different ways or methods to meditate. The choice is up to you. My primary method of meditation is a type of guided meditation by Centerpointe. This technology has done wonders for my mental health and its something that I recommend for anyone and especially for people that think meditation is hard or not something they think they can master. CenterPointe Holosync meditation simplifies the process and puts you in a meditative state a lot easier than conventional meditation. Again I have to emphasize that getting yourself to do it regularly and following instructions are the important parts.

Zazen

Twice a week I do a form of Zen mediation called Zazen. There are many forms of Zen meditation but this is very simple. The meditation is done by sitting down and focusing on your breath. By doing this practice you will gradually start feeling the calming effects and go into a deeper meditative state. If you are a martial artist then you probably use similar breathing in your practice and it should come naturally when you meditate. If you are not a martial artist then dont worry, it's a simple process to learn. However to get the full positive effects you need to be consistent in your practice.

You can the practice in the following way:

-Sit on the ground with your legs crossed. I recommend sitting on a desk chair with a straight back for beginners. This will help you focus on your breath if you are a beginner. Sitting on the floor distract beginners and scare people with injuries from mediation. So just start with a chair and if you want to move to the ground a few months later then do it.

-Try and sit upright and balanced. Posture is very important. Don't lean in any direction, sit up straight.

-Close your eyes or keep it open if you want. But I find it easier to stay focused with my eyes closed.

-Breathing is the key to this meditation. Start by taking a slow long breath in. Try to go for about 90% in.(Don't try to go as full possible)

-With the out-breath go out slow and breath out 100%

-Repeat this process and build up a rhythm with this type of breathing. Just keep your focus on your breath.

-Remember to especially focus on that out-breath and keeping it long and deliberate.

-In Zen, they say the breath in meditation is similar to the roar of a tiger.

The mind is open to all kind of suggestions consciously and unconsciously. It's easy for the mind to get overwhelmed and cluttered. When the mind gets overwhelmed and cluttered it easily gives in to instant gratification and the resistance of pain. In order to strengthen the mind, you need to implement some type of meditation into your life. Doesn't have to be long but 20-30 minutes a day is a must to clear your mind and spend some time with yourself and focus on what is important. This is the time where you get rid of all the garbage running around your mind and you get yourself back to neutral.

Don't look for instant results with meditation. This is not a quick fix. The results of meditation are subtle but you will start noticing changes after a few months of consistent practice. You will find yourself calmer, more focused and in control.

Spiritual

The modern world and especially the scientific world has been very harsh towards the religious and spiritual. Science has made vast generalizations about all spirituality and has been calling for an end to it all. This culture has grown and the importance of having a spiritual life as decreased rapidly. Interestingly enough in the countries where spirituality and religion have disappeared things like depression and unhappiness have increased.

I'm not here to encourage any specific religion or spirituality. However, I am saying that there is value in spiritual life and whatever elements or form you choose to adopt or make your own is your choice. Religion and spirituality have been with a man since the beginning of time. An internal world of stories, myths, and meaning give humans direction and stability. You don't need to believe in God or the afterlife to get value from spiritual life. But if you choose to believe in that then go for it.

The great warrior traditions have relied on religion to give them strength, hope, and courage in times of adversity. The Samurai in Japan adopted Buddhism after witnessing the extreme courage and bravery of Zen Buddhist Monks. The Samurai witnessed monks fighting and dying with no fear of death. This impressed and intrigued the Samurai.

They learned that through studying Zen and Mediation they became better warriors and had a better life. Even modern warriors pray to the universe, the force or God when they go into battle. Rationality alone is not always enough in times of extreme chaos and adversity. In times of overwhelming stress, men start breaking and then they rely on their spiritual world to share the burden. This burden sharing through meditation or prayer often make the difference between winning or losing. Between life or death.

In modern Psychology, a similar theory exist. They call it responsibility transfer. By believing in a higher force or power give men courage and self-belief. Men start performing above and beyond their capabilities. These powers get elevated through spirituality. Again, whether its real or not is irrelevant. The Results speak for itself.

Visualization

Another layer on top of meditation is visualization. Visualization is something that's also been used for thousands of years and is related to meditation but is slightly different. These days visualization is used by many successful sports teams and business professionals to get what they want out of life.

There is a famous story about how Micheal Phelps used visualization in his preparation for the Beijing Olympics and this helped him to go on and win many gold medals. You can read more about in in the famous book "The Power of Habit" by Charles Duhigg.

Phelps had a brilliant coach that taught him how to master his mind. Specifically, he taught him how to visualize. The coach called it "the videotape". He would instruct Phelps to go home and "watch the videotape" after training. The "videotape" was a visualization process where Phelps would visualize the perfect race. Every morning before getting out of bed and every night before he would sleep he would lie in bed watching the videotape. He would visualize jumping off the blocks and then in slow motion see himself executing the perfect race. He would experience the race in detail. He would feel the water on his skin and how he would rip of his goggles at the end. He would know everything about the race in his mind.

Before swimming practice, his coach would tell him to put in the "videotape". Then he would swim amazing times and keep improving..Sometimes Phelps would change the videotape by imagining things going wrong in a race but still swimming a perfect race. He would visualize how he would overcome problems if they come up in a race. For example, he trained in the dark to prepare for losing his vision in a race. He would then visualize that happening in his "videotape" and still win his race"

Combined with the visualization process was a set of core habits that Phelps would use every day. For example, stretching, eating the same thing, listing to the same music etc. When he visualized he incorporated these habits. Everything became a smooth operating machine

On Aug. 13, 2008, Phelps started his routine in Beijing . It was a big day at the Olympics and Phelps had already "put in his tape".The process has already started. By the time he hit the water, he was already 80% finished with his tape. The swim was just finishing the process. That morning as soon as he hit the water his goggles started filling with water. By the final turn, he could not see anything. He was swimming with no vision. Most other people would have started panicking and lost the race. For Phelps, it was another videotape that he has run hundreds of times. He still went on to win gold. This is a simple version of the story but it illustrates the enormous power of visualization.I recommend reading the amazing book by Charles Duhigg., "The Power Of Habit", to learn more about habits and routines and how you can combine it with visualization.

Habits

By creating strong positive habits in your life, you will make it easier for your brain to get into line in terms of what you want to achieve. In the previous part of this chapter, I talked about visualization and how Phelps used it t reach high levels of success. I also touched on the topic of habits.

The habits that Phelps used in combination with visualization is called Keystone Habits. The keystone habits are what the author Charles Duhigg refers to as habits that have the power to transform your life. Duhigg says the following of keystone habits "Keystone habits don't create a direct cause-and-effect relationship, but they can spark chain reactions that help other good habits take hold," (Charles Duhigg, The Power of Habit,2012)

Here are Examples of powerful keystone habits :
- Make your bed every morning
- Having Daily routines
- Exercising Every Day
- Planning Your Days and Weeks

Digital Declutter

The mind has never in history been exposed to so many outside stimuli. The mind has never been fed a constant stream of information like it is now. The digital and information revolution has been both a blessing and a curse. The modern tools we use like smartphones and computers are very powerful. These tools can make our lives better but can also do a lot of damage. It might be hard to spend less time on your phone. But you need a digital declutter. Schedule a day a week away from your smartphone. If you are in a position where your job requires you to always be in contact with the outside world then get a cheap dumb phone that only takes calls for emergencies. Being online 24 hours a day is not good for you.

The Big Sponge

The mind is a big sponge, and it sucks up all the information it gets. It analyzes the information without judgment. So for example, if you watch soap dramas all day long, five days a week then this will start dominating your mind. It will influence you whether you are aware of it or not.It's the same for the opposite scenario. If you focus on reading a good book every day, then those thoughts will start dominating your mind.

This goes out into all areas of our life. Like the people we surround ourselves with, the music we listen to, the movies we watch, the websites we visit and everything that we do on a consistent basis. Like I said before the mind doesn't judge, it just takes the dominant information and tries to create a reality based on that. So this represents one form of programming.

The other form is childhood programming. The things we got exposed to since birth.The things our parents did or said. The teachers, churches and other "role models" we had, and the schools we attended. Our formative years as babies and young children played a massive part in our brain development. A lot of fears, phobias, and mind patterns can be traced back to this part of our lives, and we have been running these programs for a long time.

We can take a look at a lot of issues or problems in our own lives. By looking closer we will probably see many patterns or things that we did as children that we are still doing today. In my life, there were a few patterns I was running since I was a child into my twenties. I did not even realize I was doing it because I was not aware of my mental habits. For example, the way I was speaking to my friends. Sometimes I would be rude for no reason. I had to take a step back recognize this behavior and change it. This is just a simple example of some form of bad mental habits that many of us carry with us. Another example could be reacting in a negative way when something bad happens in our lives. We can recognize this mental habit and decide to react differently next time we are in a similar situation.

The good news is we can reprogram our minds over time. It will not be easy but with consistent practice, we can make massive improvements in the way our minds operate and by doing this make huge improvements in the quality of our lives.

Change Our Mindset

Everything starts with your mindset. Carol Dweck wrote the fantastic book Mindset: The New Psychology of Success. In the book, she talks about the fixed mindset and the growth mindset. We have to remember that things don't have to be like they currently are, and we can learn and improve. Things are not set in stone. You are not who you think you are. We can all change and become better at living. It's a choice!

People with a fixed mindset will probably not read this book since they think its pointless. People with a fixed mindset think that life is the way it is and you can't change it. However, people with a growth mindset thinks you have the potential to become whoever you want if you put in the work and stay focused.

The mindset you create for yourself is important. The mindset will be the way you think and approach life. Your mindset will make or break your success.

Mindset Guidelines

The following is the mindset of a driven, successful man:

1. He Accepts responsibility for everything in his life, this includes the good and the bad.

He believes that he does not owe anyone what he would be in the future, or what he has already become. He accepts that he is responsible for his own actions because he has the awareness that everything that happens to him comes out of his free will.

To be the man that you want to become means having the power to change what you can and accept the things that you cannot, without blaming other people for untoward consequences of your actions. Responsibility for your own life means that you are capable of making your own choices. That also means that you understand that being the ultimate man does not mean that you have achieved perfection – you would still experience good and bad situations, and you should be man enough to accept that they are part of your life.

Remember that you are no longer a child. Should you encounter hardships, do not think that you should have listened to what other people said – you are a grown man capable of making your own mind. There is no one else that drove you to a bad situation apart from yourself. If you find yourself taking advantage of a good opportunity, then you also owe it to yourself. No one is responsible for your own defeats and successes. You have the sole ownership to what you can make in your life, whether it is good or bad. Starting today, think that you are a person capable of thinking for yourself without having the need for other people to make decisions. There is no choice but to accept responsibility for your own self.

2. Find your purpose and pursue it with everything that you have.

If you feel that you are driven to act and improve yourself to chase after your goals, then you have this Alpha trait. If you are aware that no one should be able to stop you from getting the things that you want as long as you keep focused, then you know that there is no way you can fail in anything that you strive to do.

Without a sense of purpose, you would be swayed from one direction to another. You would not be able to be half the man that you think you should be. If you don't know your purpose, then lock yourself in a room until you find out what your purpose is.Do whatever it takes to figure out what your purpose is.

3. He is prepared to walk alone when he goes after his purpose.

He knows that he will be criticized and opposed, and these challenges excite him. When you want to be a man that can surpass the standards of anyone that you know, you are aware that you are thinking unconventionally. That awareness that you are unlike most people should lead you into knowing that you will not be followed by everyone at the beginning. People will not buy the idea that you would succeed.But they would want to be with you once you are able to show them that you can make things work even on your own.

You need to be prepared for challenges that would come from the very people that would admire you in the future. These people would be your worst critics and your worst enemies at the beginning, but wait for it – once you are able to prove that they are wrong, they would want to root for you in the end. For this reason, think of criticism as a very exciting challenge that would give you rewards. Once you commit to your purpose and be rewarded by your hard work, you would realize that people would desire to be around you.

4. He has his own reality, and other people are guests in it. Live your life by your own rules.

If you want to reach the top, you have to have a powerful belief that the truth for you may not be the truth for others. However, you have a very high standard on what is acceptable for you. Even though you are aware that most people around you are fine with what is going on, you want to live in a culture of excellence. For that reason, you choose to live in your own reality.

While you may accommodate people in your life they need to understand that if they do not want to be part of your competitive world they are free to leave. A compromise that is designed to make you mediocre and subscribe to another person's beliefs is not an agreement that is worth your time. Remember that from now on, you are the ruler of your own life. You do not need other people's approval in choosing how you should act or making decisions for yourself.

At this point, you are embarking on an adventure that would allow you to be a king of your own realm – you are not forcing people to enter your reality, and there is no reason for them to have the right to take charge of how you should live your life. Remember that you are the only one who truly knows yourself. Only you can tell what you can do in the future.

5. He looks for discomfort and then overcomes it, he knows that this is where growth takes place.

You are aware that life is not perfect, and there may be temporary setbacks to your goals. However, no matter how uncomfortable life may become, you see every problem as an opportunity to grow.

Of course, no one wants to be in a difficult position. However, you need to see that you are going nowhere if you are unable to test your limits or if you are unable to leave anything that you do not like anymore. If you think that you are going to be rejected or that you would fail if you choose to switch careers, then you need to think if you are satisfied being an ordinary person in a position that you do not like. Surely, going after what you truly want is worth every risk. If you want to see to it that you would be able to truly achieve your goals, then you should not be afraid of a little risk in exchange for bigger rewards. You are not losing anything but your life's prison.

Once you make the decision to reach your top potential, you will have a better understanding that no man, fictional or not, has claimed that life is easy. In fact, the more you strive to move towards perfection, the more you would discover that there are difficulties that you may have not encountered in the past – the more you improve, the tougher the challenges would be. Take this realization to mean that you would no longer be bothered by small problems – the more you immerse yourself into things that cause you discomfort, the more resilient you become.

6. Self-improvement is a part of his life until he dies.

A man with a warrior mindset believes in the concept of Kaizen, the Japanese belief that all things in the world are capable of being endlessly improved.

While you may understand that there is no way that the world that you are in can be perfect, aiming for constant and consistent improvement grants you the ideal that every situation or object in your reality can become better. By embodying this principle, you would have the peace of mind that even though you fall behind and make mistakes, you are capable of being able to fix what is broken and even make them work to your advantage. Because you believe that all things can be improved, you will want to find how you can make use of the resources that are around you.

Because you believe that you would be a better version of yourself, you would put your progress into a test. You would stop relying on others and discipline yourself to achieve your goals no matter what. After all, you have the certainty that the things that you cannot do today are the things that you would be able to do in the near future.

At this point, you have the understanding that your aim is to continuously improve all aspects of your life, no matter how difficult it can be.

7. Self-Education is very important to him.

He reads a lot and listens to audio programs to learn about a wide variety of subjects like psychology, self-help, philosophy, history, and evolution. This process of learning continues forever.

Successful men will find a way to continue learning, within or outside the walls of the academy. This is a true trait of most corporate leaders in the world, which makes it a point to read at least 5 books in a month. That means that even though these men were able to reach the peak of their careers, they still make it a point to continue their education through reading. The reason is simple – the extra knowledge that they may gain today can become a very useful skill that they can use should they find themselves wanting to immerse in another field of interest.

8. He controls his Mind and Emotions.

He uses meditation, breathing, and physical movement to make sure he is in a constant state of positive energy. He does not allow negative emotions to dominate his mind. He recognizes that negativity is part of life, and then immediately gets rid of negative emotions. Depressed people stay in negative states, he never does because he deals with it. That is the difference, he does not live in negative states of mind; he recognizes it, and then deals with it and moves on to the positive state of mind.

The Succesful man is capable of maintaining his composure no matter what his environment is. The reason why he makes it a point to have a sound mind and heart, no matter how challenging the circumstances are is simple – clouded minds make clouded judgments, which he would never want to make. He aims to make logical and fair judgment all the time because it is the only way for him to make decisions.

This is where the training to become Self Disciplined becomes hard – right now, it may seem impossible for you to get your emotions grounded during a difficult time. It is very hard to think right when you are under pressure. You think that because it is very uncomfortable to be on the spot, you need to make a decision right away even when you are still uncertain of what you should do. Don't rush yourself –

clear your mind first and once you are able to become calm, consider all the options that are laid out in front of you.

9. He has a mindset of winning.

He always approaches life from the mindset that he has already won. He visualized his victories before it happens. This is his reality.

There is no way for any person to achieve success in an instant. However, there is a way to plan success by taking goals one piece at a time. An Alpha understands that while he cannot teleport right into the goal that he wants to reach, he can devise a roadmap to success that would allow him to reach his destination in the most efficient way possible.

To do this, you need to first believe that no matter how daunting your goal is, you would be able to still reach it. All you need to do is to think about how you are going to trim down a goal into small, more actionable targets and then take them one by one. Make sure that you are able to mark your progress as you go to feel motivated as you go along the way. Should you hit a roadblock to your progress, you can make minor revisions to your plan in order to find the right tactic to hit a particular goal.

10. He has a sense of humor in adversity.

The Elite British Royal Marines Commandos has a principle that every Marine Commando has to learn. The rule is "Cheerfulness in the face of adversity".The Royal Marines Commandos know that reframing adversity in their minds and seeing the funny side of the whole situation gives them a mental edge. It creates powerful positive energy that pushes them through any level of adversity.

The successful man realizes that sometimes he should just laugh and see the funny side when things get tough. Difficult times often make a man feel down. However, a true man understands that when failure and disaster strikes, not everything is lost. He knows he can frame any situation in his mind so that he can see the funny side in it. He knows humor creates positive energy.

Looking at the funny side of things does great wonders. Not only do you avoid preventable stress, you also make use of your faculties to enable you to make better use of your time. By recognizing that you made a mistake and then quickly shrugging it off, your brain starts to process what you should have done and how you are going to make up for the mistake that you just committed. Having the ability to laugh at mistakes also allows you to regain your focus, which helps you quickly recover from a mishap.

11. He has Accepted death.

He does not hide from it and does not fear it. He thinks of it every day and this inspires him to live life to its fullest. He learned this from the ancient samurai tradition that thinks about death in the morning when they get up so they can get inspired to live a full and rich life every day.

Appreciating life and the opportunity to live for one more day inspires you to do what you can to improve yourself and the lives of people around you for the limited time that you have in this world. Once you have accepted that you would face death in a way that you do not expect, you would make it a point to live your life in ways that you never did in the past. It also makes you realize that there is so much that you still want to accomplish, and there is no better day to make dreams come true but today.

Once you adopt the principle of not fearing death, you would observe how much courage you gain – you become undaunted by the chance of failure, as long as you have measurable means to success. At the same time, you are motivated to improve and achieve as much as you can every day – you desire to learn more and start projects that you have shelved. Everything becomes important. Once you embrace the fact that you would possibly die tomorrow, you want each day to feel like you are about to leave a legacy behind.

12. He never complains.

Complaining is a waste of energy, especially if you are still in a position wherein you need to go back to work and fix an error. Complaining puts your motivation down, and once you think that there is nothing else that you can do about the situation and somebody else should be doing the fixing, then you are creating an even bigger problem than the situation itself. You are creating an infectious mindset that prevents people from thinking of solutions, and then induces a blaming marathon that would never end.

If you have the habit of complaining, ask yourself this question: is the task that you need to do so difficult that it exists outside your skill set? If you answer No to this question, then there is no reason to complain – just go ahead and do it already. Only incapable people whine.

13. He has incredibly high standards in life. He never compromises on these standards in all areas of life.

If you feel that you are never satisfied, then you already have the makings of being successful. Satisfaction becomes the end of curiosity and the start of making do with what exists around you. However, if you have the itch to continue improving all the details that you see in your reality for the benefit of everyone that belongs to your world, then you know that you have higher standards than everyone else.

Ordinary men will make do with what they have – they will be fine with the wage that an employer gives them, without even asking what they need to do to deserve a raise. They will be fine with the fact that there are other people that earn less than two dollars in a day, as long as they are content with the idea that they can pay rent. They are fine with the knowledge that less than a percent of the population actually owns all the industries in the world, and they are not part of that statistic.

If you are greatly disturbed by what is happening around you and you want to work for change, then that is a good thing. Because you feel annoyed or irritated with what is happening with the world, you are compelled to take action, compared to those that are simply saddened that injustice happens around them and they cannot do anything about it. When you have that itch for change, you would do whatever it takes to get that feeling out of your skin.

14. He sets massive goals and goes after them. He does not give up until he reaches his goals.

A successful man live by the challenge of his goals – achieving goals and setting up personal challenges is both a habit and a hobby to him. Since Alphas are fond of discovering their current limits and how they can surpass them in the most efficient way possible, they also make it a point that they set massive goals. The more daunting they are, the better they sound.

Massive goals, no matter what they are, are still actionable as long as you can think of the best way to churn them down. Now, the churning down of these goals serves as an exciting hobby for an alpha – for example, he may see himself becoming the CEO of a very lucrative company, but he needs to lay out a roadmap made up of small, actionable, and timely goals to make this goal come true.

As he creates this plan, he is excited on taking all those steps as he thought it, and every time he succeeds, he becomes even more motivated to take the next one. Because he loves the feeling of being successful, he also becomes very excited in other large prospects that he has in mind. The achievement of massive goals gives him the power that he craves, and that is the knowledge that he can dictate what should happen to his life.

15. Fitness and health is one of his priorities.

He goes to the gym lift weights and does yoga for flexibility. He eats healthy and takes high-quality supplements to manage the demands of his lifestyle.

The secret to a great physique is simple: he considers his body and his mind as tools for success. For that reason, he sees to it that he gives his body the same attention that he does to his mind. He makes it a point that he is always in top shape to not only look presentable to other people but to also allow him to do more in a day.

Successful men consider fatigue as one of the enemies of achieving daily progress, and in order to eliminate that factor altogether, he makes it a point that he focuses on strengthening exercises. He also sees to it that he only eats healthy food that boosts his mind and body. He also does not get tempted with decadent food, alcohol, and illegal substances– he knows that to consume them is to make his body and mind less functional, thus delaying him in achieving his next target.

16. Self-Discipline.

Self- Discipline in life is his cornerstone. Discipline is reached by consistency in actions and not compromising on goals.

At the heart of every successful man is that unwavering discipline – he is a military unit on his own, and he believes that in order to win life battles, he needs to make sure that all his faculties are doing what is planned. Because he has his goals set in stone, there is no way that he could be tempted by the little devils of an ordinary man, like hitting the snooze button in the morning or having that extra shot of tequila when he has to wake up early.

Alphas know that in order to experience abundance, he has to figure out a way to avoid excess. He knows that before he takes control of other people and situations, he has to figure out how he can control himself.

7

The Body

Now that we covered the mind its time to move on to the body and everything that influences it.Although the body and mind is part of one big machine we will discuss it as a separate part of who you are. The following components will make you perform at optimal levels:

Exercise

You have to implement physical exercise at least 5 days a week. You can take a break on weekends if you have to but weekdays are non-negotiable. Personally, I do 6 days on and one day off. But if you are a beginner in this world of Self Discipline then start with 5.

We are all busy people but we need to take time for physical training. This should be non-negotiable. I have listed 3 different types of physical training.There are many forms of exercise, however, in my opinion, these 3 gives you the most n return as an investment. For me there are no better forms of physical exercise than following:

(1)Weight Training

(2)Yoga

(3)Running

(1)Weight Training

Weight training has to be the foundation for building a strong healthy body. Focus on the traditional compound exercises. These are bench press, dead-lift, squats, and shoulder presses. Then add body weight exercises like pull ups and push ups and burpees.

Like I said before even if you are not a "gym person" then become one. Get over yourself and look at the big picture. The big picture is that weight training is the best way to build strength, build muscle, burn fat, boost testosterone and improve your overall health.

Sometimes weight training gets a bad rap from some health circles. However, the latest science concludes that the benefits of weight training are incredible and gives you the best bang for your buck. The latest studies also show that weight lifting is a superior option to cardio when it comes to burning fat and losing weight.

According to the MAYO Clinic you will get the following benefits from Weight training:

(1)Develop Stronger bones over time.

(2)Keep your weight in check

(3)Increase your Stamina

(4)Manage and Reduce the Symptoms of Chronic conditions

(5)Improve your focus and attention.

If I had to choose one form of exercise, then it would be weight training. Even if get forced to do only two exercises it would be dead-lifts and squats. With just those two exercises I would be able to stay healthy and strong

The vital hormones like testosterone that all males need get boosted when we lift weights and this is crucial when it comes to a man's health.With the environment changing and influencing our health we need our hormones to operate on an optimum level. Weight training is one of the ways that help us boost those hormones. But more on the importance of hormones later.

How do I get started with weight training?

The obvious part is to join a gym. However, the most important part is to have a plan and to stick with it.

Most people give up on training because they don't have a plan, so they get no results. Then they lose motivation and quit. Where to get a plan? Well, there are hundreds of good workout plans online to check out. Or check out my blog for some resources. You can get some workout plans for about $15- 20. It's worth it to spend some money on your body. It is an investment in yourself.

(2)Stretching/Yoga

I do Yoga twice a week to stretch out my body and keep me flexible and injury free. It's also a great form of meditation.

Many guys won't even consider the idea of Yoga, but Yoga is one of the most valuable ways to improve your body and mind The benefits to your overall flexibility and strength are huge, not to mention the effect on your mind. It will help you deal with stress in a lot more efficient way.

Forget about Yoga classes where there is a hippie talking about the afterlife. There are many different types of yoga that will give you a kickass workout. As I said, the best classes are the ones where you get a good physical workout with a good teacher that is not full of crap.

If you are walking into a class and someone wants to cleanse your aura, walk out and find another school. There are many, and you can sit down and watch a class as an observer before you sign up for classes.

One of my favorite books on Yoga is written by a Navy SEAL, and I highly recommend you check it out. The book is called Kokoro Yoga by Mark Divine, and this book has all the tools to get you started and transform your life. One of the awesome parts of the book is the section on how to manage your breathing.

Benefits following a Yoga session:

Improves brain functioning.
    Even for only twenty to thirty minutes of Hatha yoga can help enhance cognition and improve concentration as well as memory. This type of yoga is focused more on physical postures as compared to others which emphasize sequences or flow.

Decreases levels of stress.
    According to a recent study conducted in the University of California, yoga has the capacity to reduce the action of proteins that are known to contribute in engendering inflammation.

Modifies gene expression.
    Research study in Norway indicated that the numerous health

benefits of this practice possibly come from its capability to modify gene expression in the body's immune cells.

Improves flexibility.

Bikram Yoga involves a total of 26 postures that are supposed to be accomplished within ninety minutes inside a heated venue. According to a study conducted by the Colorado State University, this kind of activity is associated to more flexibility in the lower back, shoulder, and hamstring. In addition, increased muscle strength and lesser body fat were observed.

Benefits following months of practice:

Decreases blood pressure.

Individuals who are hypertensive could benefit from yoga exercises. A study found that this activity is more effective in lowering blood pressure as comparison to those who engaged in other activities such as walking, counseling programs to lose weight, and nutrition.

Increases lung capacity.

Vital lung capacity increases after weeks of engaging in regular Hatha Yoga. Vital lung capacity which is a component of lung capacity refers to the greatest amount of air that may be expired after deep inspiration of air.

Enhances sexual function.

Yoga has demonstrated that it can increase a person's sexual desire and sexual satisfaction. Through yoga, women are able to familiarize themselves with their bodies and the extent of their capabilities.

Decreases chronic pain in the neck.

Iyengar Yoga emphasizes correct alignment and usage of supportive equipment during activity. Weeks of engaging in this exercise can help decrease intense pain among individuals suffering from chronic neck pain.

Alleviates chronic back pain.
Iyengar Yoga helps in enhancing mood and decreasing pain particularly with those who have difficulties with their lower back.

Help maintain blood sugar levels among diabetics.
Regular yoga practice can help in reducing weight and steadying levels of blood sugar.

Increases sense of balance.
The elderly or people over the age of 65 years usually experience problems with their sense of balance. With regular practice of yoga, this can be improved to avoid falls among elderly people.

Benefits following years of yoga practice:

Help develop stronger bones.
It is typical for the elderly to decrease bone density and bones becoming brittle. However, with yoga practice, they can improve their bone mineral density or gain bone.

Helps in reducing and maintaining an appropriate weight.
A research group from Seattle found a relation between regular yoga and reduced or properly maintained weight among thousands of healthy personalities. The overweight people who have regular exercise lost more or less five pounds at the time while those who are not gained.

Reduces risk of a heart ailment.
Yoga as one of the modifying changes people integrate into their lives may help in decreasing the risk of cardiac problems like high

levels of cholesterol and sugar in the blood including hypertension.

Different Types of Yoga and Finding the Best One For You

Ashtanga Yoga.

A total of six sequences comprised of an array of postures usually instructed one position at a time. The majority of the sessions concentrate on what is referred to as the Primary Series. This is not so complicated for new participants but may be difficult for persons who have not started to exercise. Students learn in different phases, with the instructor helping out and teaching new poses while old ones are mastered.

Bikram Yoga.

This class involves accomplishing all 26 poses and 2 breathing exercises. Each one is held for one whole minute and is done two times. The class is held in a heated room and does not use music.

Hatha Yoga.

This is a slow and gentle type of yoga class that is well suited for beginners, people with mobility issues.

Iyengar Yoga.

This concentrates on the alignment of the body. Poses are meticulously instructed. Props like blankets, blocks, chairs, and straps may be used for the different poses. Each one is held longer as compared to other yoga classes. Classes are slowly paced and strict; however, students are assured to learn a lot. This fits well with any age, beginners, and people recuperating from any physical injury.

Power Yoga.

The classes are highly dynamic and sporty. It is a form of Ashtanga that turned western style. It started to use other various poses aside from those used in Ashtanga. This yoga activity has added moves that strengthen muscles particularly the core muscles. There are many poses accompanied by regulated breathing in between with lots of strength-building poses, pushups, and handstands. This is not suitable for individuals with limited mobility or injury and who would rather join in gentle yoga sessions.

Vinyasa Yoga.

This has a more rapid pace flow classes. They can cross over different schools of yoga and may move faster. This is great for individuals who easily get tired of the same routine they perform regularly.

Practicing Yoga At Home

Practicing yoga at home can save money, energy, and time. At the same time, no stranger or another person who will be looking at your behind as you execute the different poses required in class. A half hour of yoga at home is frequently more advantageous than driving yourself to a studio, searching for a spot to park, and others cashing in for every session you attend.

(3)Cardio

The biggest reason people fail with running is the lack of consistency and the absence of a plan.

Get Started

You've been hearing a lot of good things about running: how it has helped people lose a lot of weight, how it makes people feel good and accomplished, has lowered people's blood pressure, cholesterol levels, and so on. You want to try it out yourself, but you are not sure whether you are ready for it. You feel like you don't know where to begin.

If this is the feeling that you have right now, there's only one thing that you need to do: start shopping.

That's right. The first step to running is to shop for the right running shoes. Doesn't sound so hard, does it? If you already have running gear, buy an extra pair of socks. Signaling your mind that you are investing on something is a great motivator to get you started.

Follow a Beginner's Program

Now that you have your running shoes, you are probably really excited to get started. Nevertheless, there are few guidelines that you need to know first before you begin:

Start by walking. Running is an intense exercise, which means that you need to give your body time to adapt first. Walking will let your heart and muscles warm up and gradually increase. After putting your shoes on, start walking for about 30 minutes on flat terrain, then go home and reflect on how it made you feel. If it was effortless, then you are ready to kick it up a notch tomorrow.

The Beginner Runner's Schedule. Beginners are advised to go out there for 30 minutes a day, four days per week. This 30 minutes is not dedicated entirely to running; it can be a combination of running and walking.

Keep in mind that you will feel soreness and discomfort the following day after you run, which is why you need to start with walking first. In order to help you ease into the program, here is a running schedule meant for beginners (you will need a timer):

1st Week:

Day 1: Walk for 10 minutes. In the next 10 minutes, switch between running for 1 minute and walking for 1 minute. Spend the last 10 minutes walking.

Day 2: Walk for 10 minutes. In the next 15 minutes, switch between running for 1 minute and walking for 1 minute. Spend the last 5 minutes walking.

Day 3: Walk for 10 minutes. In the next 15 minutes, switch between running for 2 minutes and walking for 1 minute. Spend the last 5 minutes walking.

Day 4: Walk for 5 minutes. In the next 21 minutes, switch between running for 2 minutes and walking for 1 minute. Spend the last 4 minutes walking.

2nd Week:

Day 1: Walk for 5 minutes. In the next 20 minutes, switch between running for 3 minutes and walking for 1 minute. Spend the last 5 minutes walking.

Day 2: Walk for 5 minutes. In the next 21 minutes, switch between running for 5 minutes and walking for 2 minutes. Spend the last 4 minutes walking.

Day 3: Walk for 4 minutes. In the next 24 minutes, switch between running for 5 minutes and walking for 1 minute. Spend the last 2 minutes walking.

Day 4: Walk for 5 minutes. In the next 22 minutes, switch between running for 8 minutes and walking for 3 minute. Spend the last 3 minutes walking.

3rd Week:

Day 1: Walk for 5 minutes. Follow it with 10 minutes of running. Walk for 5 minutes after that. Run for another 5 minutes. Spend the last 5 minutes walking.

Day 2: Walk for 5 minutes. Follow it with 12 minutes of running. Walk for 5 minutes after that. Run for another 5 minutes. Spend the last 5 minutes walking.

Day 3: Walk for 10 minutes. Run for 15 minutes. Spend the last 5 minutes walking.

Day 4: Walk for 6 minutes. Run for 18 minutes. Spend the last 6 minutes walking.

4th Week:

Day 1: Walk for 5 minutes. Run for 20 minutes. Spend the last 5 minutes walking.

Day 2: Walk for 5 minutes. Run for 22 minutes. Spend the last 3 minutes walking.

Day 3: Walk for 3 minutes. Run for 25 minutes. Spend the last 2 minutes walking.

Day 4: Run for 30 minutes.

Stretching and Running Techniques

Most people think that running is just about putting one foot in front of the other really fast. However, there is more behind the science of running than that. Knowing the different running techniques will help improve your overall running experience and let you boost your speed, form and progress efficiently.

Always Stretch before you Run. Well-stretched muscles will ensure that you will have a great running workout because they will not be fatigued or sore afterwards. Not stretching can also lead to injury, which will further hinder you from doing your workouts regularly.

Here are the 10 steps on how to do a basic warm-up stretches. The entire routine will not take more than 5 minutes.

Step 1: Wall Push ups

Base position: Stand three feet from the wall with feet in line with shoulders and flat on the floor. Place your hands against the walls with arms straight.

Lean hips forward, then bend knees slightly. Feel the stretch in your calf muscles. Repeat 3 times.

Next, resume base position. Bend your torso forward to waist height. Lift one foot forward with knee slightly bent. Lift the toes. Feel the stretch in the muscles under the calf. Repeat 3 times. Do the same for the other leg.

Resume base position. Put feet together and stand on your heels with arms straight to form a jackknife shape. Feel the stretch in your hips, shoulders and lower back. Repeat 3 times.

Step 2: Back Scratch

Hold your left elbow using your right hand and slowly push your elbow upwards and across the body until your left hand touches down your back, as if to scratch it. Slowly push your left elbow to bring the hand as far down as comfortable for you. Feel the stretch in your triceps and shoulders. Repeat 3 times and change arm.

Step 3: Hamstring Stretch

Lie flat on the floor. Bring your left leg straight up while keeping your right leg positioned with knee bent and foot flat on the floor. Loop an old towel over the arch of your left foot and slowly pull on it to push against the foot. Keep pulling until you feel the muscles in your leg contract. Repeat 3 times and change foot.

Step 4: Quadriceps Stretch

Kneel on the floor, but keep soles pointing upwards. While keeping your body straight and your arms to your side, lean back gradually and hold the position for 15 counts.

Step 5: Heel to Buttock Stretch

Stand on your left foot and keep yourself in balance by placing your right hand against a wall. Hold your right foot using your left hand and gradually lift the heel of your right foot to your buttocks. Keep your body straight throughout the process. Repeat 3 times and change foot. Feel the stretch in your quadriceps.

Step 6: Hip and Lower Back Stretch

Sit on the floor and cross your legs. Bring your right leg up and cross it over the left. Keep your left leg bent. Hug your right leg and bring it close to your chest. Twist your torso to look over your right shoulder. Hold for 8 seconds. Repeat with the other leg.

Step 7: Iliotibial Band Stretch

Lie down on your side and bring both legs bent as if in running position. Position lower leg toward the chest and position the upper leg back toward the buttocks as far as both legs can go. Hold for 30 counts before switching to the other side.

Step 8: Hamstring and Back Stretch

Lie down on your back and keep knees bent. Use your arms to bring your shins close to your chest. Hold for 30 counts.

Step 9: Bridge

Lie on your back with your feet flat on the floor. Bring your hips upwards to create a straight plane. Hold for 30 seconds and repeat 10 times. Feel the stretch in your quads and lower back.

Step 10: Groin Stretch

Sit on the ground with the soles of your feet placed together. Hold your ankles and keep your elbows on the inside of your knees. Slowly lean forward while gently pressing your knees to the ground. Push as low as what is comfortable for you. Hold for 15 counts.

The Right Pace

When you run, you think you will get out of breath. This is not true. In fact, if you huff and puff as you run, it means that you are going too fast. The right way to run should be at a relaxed and moderate pace that will train your body without going too far.

The right pace should get your heart rate up to approximately 70 percent of its maximum. But you naturally won't be able to monitor that as your run. Instead, what you implement is the Talk Test. You will know if your pace is correct when you can still talk in complete sentences while running.

The Right Form

Running is an individual sport, which means that people tend to develop their own unique technique on how to run better. The right form is basically the kind that makes you feel most comfortable as you run. Nevertheless, there are some basic safety rules that you can apply to avoid injury:

Keep your head, shoulders, torso, and pelvis upright and aligned.

Look ahead, not down on the ground.

Shoulders should be relaxed, with the arms carried just below the chest.

Hands should be relaxed, cupped loosely and passes the body at approximately waist level.

Arms should move in sync with the legs. They should move forward, instead of side to side.

Feet should land lightly beneath your center of gravity.

How to Breathe while Running

The more intense your running is, the more shallow and rapid your breathing will be. Just like your muscles, your lungs also need to train in order to boost their endurance. Also, breathing correctly will bring in more oxygen for the muscles.

Chest breathing is the incorrect way to breathe because it tenses the shoulders and wastes more energy. In fact, the true key to breathing correctly is called abdominal breathing. Wherein the abdomen should fill up like a balloon as you breathe in and deflate like a balloon as you breathe out.

As much as possible, breathe through your mouth because this allows for more oxygen to enter your lungs compared to your nostrils. However, this can sometimes cause a dry throat, so remember to swallow a bit in order to let your saliva lubricate your pharynx.

You should also coordinate your breathing by counting as you breathe. Beginners should start with a 2-2 pattern, wherein you breathe in for two steps forward and breathe out for another two steps forward. Slowly increase it to 3-3 and then to 4-4 as you improve your endurance.

The Hard-Easy Principle

This is a popular, albeit controversial, running technique that basically means alternating your running days between hard and easy. To be more specific, you run fast or longer than usual in one day of running, and then on the day after that you run shorter or slower than usual. To keep it balanced, you can start the week off at your usual pace and distance. The second day should then be your "hard" day, the third will be your "easy" day, and the fourth will get you back on your regular running day.

Striders

When you apply the striders (also known as the "pick-up") technique, you are training your muscles and nervous system to adapt to a fast pace without causing fatigue because it is so short.

Striders is not a difficult workout. In fact, you can incorporate it into your run about one to two times a week. It starts off with you running easy and then increasing your speed and lengthening your stride for around 15 seconds before you slow back down to a walk.

Here are the steps on how to do Striders for beginners. If this is your first time, you can start striding for 4 seconds and gradually build it up to 6 or 8 over time.

Step 1: Look for a flat surface that will enable you to run for 30 seconds at speed (approximately 250 to 300 feet).
   Step 2: Start running easy, concentrating on a fast but short stride.
   Step 3: Gradually build up your speed and lengthening your stride. Make sure that your upper body stays relaxed but straight. The feeling should be more of a moderated but fast pace instead of a sprint.
   Step 3: Once you are 3/4 of your way into the distance, gradually

lower your speed by shortening your stride until you drop down to a walk.

Step 4: Walk back to where you started striding while breathing steadily.

Step 5: Repeat the strider again.

Don't forget to do your striders, especially if you are planning to join a marathon. After all, striders is the best way to help you run faster and more smoothly.

How to Overcome Runner's Aches and Pains

Pain is inevitable in any sport. You Otherwise, always at some point experience some type of body issue, especially if you are just starting. Injuries are not fun at all, and the worst part is that it will prevent you from running.

Most injuries are triggered when the runner exerts too much effort too soon. It also comes from not listening to the body's danger signals. While pain is normal, injuries can be avoided.

<u>**Tips on How to Avoid Injuries while Running**</u>

Strengthen your body's ability to tolerate the repetitive forces that come with running by doing the following:

Stretching all of the major tendons, ligaments and muscles that you use while running.

Wearing the right apparel, such as runner's shoes that have adequate cushioning and are appropriate for your foot size and type, and clothes that are not constricting blood flow.

Increasing your intensity and mileage at a gradual pace in order to allow the body to adapt.

Running on soft ground whenever you can, such as dirt and grass.

Following a running program that is suitable for your level (in your case, the beginner's program) in order to avoid overexertion.

Stay Motivated

Running doesn't just happen; you have to make an effort to stick to it. There will be times when you are excited to lace up and head on out. But there are also times when you just don't feel it. While it's alright to take a rest every now and then, the sad part about thinking that you are too tired to run is that you eventually become demotivated.

Many people have turned running into their passion, and they, too, experience feeling too bored or tired to go outside and run. However, they have overcome this obstacle because they know how to get inspired.

8

Lifestyle And Nutrition

Nutrition

The old saying that we are what we eat is one of the best ways to describe how important it is that we manage what we put in our bodies. Now I'm not saying count calories, but I am saying start reading labels. Most of us have no idea what we are putting into our bodies.

The reality of modern life is that we are influenced by the environment more than ever before. Pollution has reached record levels, and the soil we grow our foods in are depleted of nutrients. So the food we eat is less nutritious than before.

Large companies and commercial farming have also influenced the way animals are bred on farms and what they eat. These animals end up on our dinner plates. We eat them without a second thought.

I just mentioned a couple of general observations about plants and animals, but what about processed food? Well, the general rule is that almost all of it is terrible for you. There are a few exceptions but not many. We pick these things up at supermarkets, and we eat them, and they taste great. They taste great because they were engineered by scientists to taste great. Big companies pay top dollar to make sure you get foods that are designed to make your hungry again 20 minutes later. These types of foods create chaos in our bodies.

If you look at the modern rates of cancer, diabetes, and other modern diseases(find examples), then we can easily find the connection between how humans have started to eat in the last 100 years. Asian cultures like Japan has a better record than us because of their food culture.

Hormones

One of the reasons society seems out of control sometimes is that there are very few people that have studied their own bodies. Our bodies are ancient and complex. The human body is capable of extraordinary things, however, like any other system, it gets damaged if we push it into the red sometimes. This is what we as a society do all the time, and we sometimes seem surprised when we get sick, feel depressed or feel like we are getting old.

Sure we are getting older and yes we sometimes just get sick. However, we have allowed our environment to influence us on a very deep level by consistently living out of balance. This balance in our body is the hormones that we have in our body. When they get out of balance, all kinds of hell brakes loose.

- **Estrogen**

Over the last 30 years, men have been getting an excess of the female hormone estrogen into their bodies. Commercial farming plastic and other factors have contributed to this.

According to Scientific Studies, there are many dangers to excess

estrogen:

(1) Man boobs or enlarged breasts. This is why we so many men with saggy boobs walking around.

(2) Low Sex Drive

(3) If you are struggling to get it up, then you could have excess estrogen.

(4) The risk of Strokes because of blood clots.

(5) Heart attack. This use to be a problem with older men but is becoming more common in younger men. Less testosterone and too much estrogen could damage the heart.

(6) Problems with the prostate.

(7) Low tolerance for stress.

We need some Estrogen in the male body, but an excess will cause an imbalance in the body, and then lead to disease.

- **Testosterone**

The most important male hormone is Testosterone. The importance of this hormone cannot be overstated. In the book Man 2.0 Engineering the Alpha by John Romaniello and Adam Bornstein, they emphasize the importance of this hormone by saying, "Testosterone is what makes you a man. It's what allows you to build muscle and build fat. It's what makes you attractive to women, what powers your sex drive and what helps you recover from workouts."

The lack of testosterone is a cause of social issues in many men's lives. If you are testosterone deficient, then it could lead to problems in our relationships, health, careers and overall happiness in life. So the importance cannot be overstated.

How do we change our eating habits, balance our hormones and improve our health?

The first thing we have to do is to change our mindset about health and wellness. In modern life, most people tend to treat symptoms when they get sick. When they feel better, they just go back to the way they lived before. I suggest we should live healthily and prevent disease. What the modern world do at the moment is treating symptoms and not the cause. This is why people keep getting sick. The medication is just masking underlying problems connected to lifestyle.

How Do We Prevent Disease and Illness?

1- Exercise

We already looked at weight training and a good form of exercise, but there are many others. Find one and start exercising consistently.

2 - Food

Well, let's start by saying that there will be some guys that will say that eating junk food is cheaper and that it's more convenient than cooking every night.

Firstly eating healthy might be a bit more expensive but the long term investment in your health and your overall improvement in your life will be worth it. If you can spend a lot of money on alcohol, then you can take that money and invest it in your health.

What should I eat?

What you put into your body is one of the most important things that you do every day. The food you eat become the building blocks of your body and this will affect the way you feel and how efficient your body functions.

If you get your diet right consistently you will perform better in all other areas of life. There are many gurus with different opinions on what is healthy.I will share with you what worked for me and then you can go try it out:

-Eat Real Food And Drink Lots Of Water

Stop Eating Processed Food Including Sugar. You might struggle to cut sugar if you have been eating it for years. However, if you get over the initial cravings your health will improve and you will lose weight. Avoid processed food with the exception of whey protein.

-Drink Loads Of Black Coffee

Don't believe the bad hype coffee had over the years. Real black coffee made from fresh coffee beans is good for you. Of course, its only good for you if you don't put in the sugar and milk. So avoid the latte and other sugary coffee drinks. Drink your coffee black. After a few weeks of black coffee and no sugar, you will never drink sugar again.

-Eat Lots of Meat

Eat a lot of good quality grass-fed meat. Most of us can't hunt deer every week and get wild meat so we have to settle for grass-fed beef or lamb. If you can't afford grass-fed go for organic or just get the best meat you can. Dont believe modern propaganda.Men need meat and lots of it. A recent study found that depression rates to be higher among vegetarians than meat eaters.so make sure you get your steak every week. Contrary to popular belief animal fats from good sources are good for you.

The foundation of your diet should be fresh and organic meat, eggs, butter and berries. I know everyone can't get or afford organic food, but don't use that as an excuse to eat crap. If you can't find organic, then eat normal meat, eggs, and fruits, it's still a lot better than processed food. Vegetables are overrated.

My diet consists mostly of the following Foods:

-Beef, Pork
    -White Rice
    -Eggs
    -Grass Fed Unsalted Butter
    -Frozen Strawberries, Blackberries , Blueberries
    -Whey Protein

You will need extra carbohydrates. My personal choice is white rice. It is reasonably healthy and will give you the extra carbs you need to deal with doing weight training.

Avoiding Soy

Soy is one of the worst things a man can out in his body. It disrupts testosterone production and spikes the production of estrogen the female hormone.

Bulletproof

One of the biggest changes in my overall health happened when I read the book the Bullet Proof Diet by Dave Asprey. His book is revolutionary in the way he scientifically approaches what we put in our bodies and how we can best optimize our health and wellness. The Bulletproof diet is most famous for the coffee and butter that made it famous. What I can say about the Bulletproof diet is that my health has never been better.

The Bulletproof diet is easy to implement, and it will improve the quality of your life.

Upgrading your nutrition goes hand in hand with exercise and like exercise is a cornerstone of a quality life. Making a big change in your eating plans can seem like a big challenge regarding implementing new habits into your life and spending extra money. However your health is a priority, and you will see the benefits in all other areas of your life like your work, relationships, and overall happiness.

- **3 -Supplements**

- You have to invest in high-quality supplements

I mentioned earlier the importance of regulating our hormones for optimum health. One of the reasons why we are so out of balance as men are our hormones are all messed up. They are messed up because of environmental factors and bad nutrition. This is where supplements come into the game. Why do we take supplements if we are already eating healthy? Well, like mentioned before our environment is messed up and the soil is depleted. So we need to boost our nutrition levels.

Not all supplements are equal and some a very bad for you. Avoid all multivitamins and focus on buying high quality supplements. It might be a bit more pricey but its worth it.

The following supplements are the essentials:

Vitamin D
  Magnesium
  Vitamin K2
  Vitamin C
  Iodine
  Krill Oil
  Vitamin A
  Zinc
  B12

If you are in doubt about supplements or can't afford high-quality supplements then rather go without them.

Whey Protein
  Whey protein is one of the few "muscle building" supplements that actually works and that is good for your overall health. Try and get grasses way or a high-quality brand with no soy.

Drink Less Alcohol

One of the obvious things to improve your health is to quit alcohol or reduce it. I have almost totally cut alcohol from my life and my life has totally transformed. I still drink a glass of red wine on special occasions but that is it.

Fasting
  Intermittent fasting is one of the best things you can do to improve your overall health. Intermittent fasting has many benefits but lets' look at a few. For example, when you fast your body initiates important cellular repair processes. Fasting also changes hormone levels to make stored body fat more accessible. Some studies have shown intermittent fasting may enhance the body's resistance to oxidative

stress. One more thing intermittent fasting will test is your mind. There is no better test that Intermittent fasting to see how strong your self-discipline is. Your mind and body will try and get you to start eating, but you have to overcome this and focus on your physical goals.

9

The Martial Way

If you have no experience in Japanese martial arts then you have probably never heard of the term Budō. Budō is a Japanese philosophy and a way of life that uses Martial Arts as a path of self-improvement. Budō can be traced back to the 17th century Japan. Back then the Samurai had come to a strange point in their evolution as a warrior class. Through many years of training as a way of life, they have come to the point where most Samurai was almost perfect swordsman. This created the problem of getting the better of your opponent.

The Samurai had already incorporated Zen into their culture by late in the 13th century. Zen meditation gave them the skill of intense focus and overcoming the fear of death. By the 17 century, Budō started to appear in the Samurai culture.

The Samurai came to the conclusion that the warriors with the superior mental and spiritual attitude were the ones that were consistently victorious. This is how Budō developed as a way of life.

Budō is the way of the warrior. All Japanese Martial arts has its roots in Budō. We can say that Budō explores through direct experience and in depth the relationship between ethics, philosophy, and religion. Budō is a way of life. Its a way of self - development, and self-exploration.

Modern Sports martial arts is not Budō. Sports martial arts has 3 aspects that are different from Budō:

(1) The goal with a sport is to determine a winner and loser. Competitors try to get medals or trophies.

(2) Sports have rules. If there were no rules then it would end with fights to the death.

(3) There are umpires to enforce the 'rules.'

So what about Budō?

Well, none of these rules exist. Of course, Budō practitioners want to be victorious but that is not the end goal. Budō is not a game and sword fights started the moment the duel was decided.

From thee moment the duel was decided the warriors were starting to take actions to defeat their opponents. There is a famous story about the legendary Samurai Miyamoto Musashi. From the moment the time and date were set all kinds of battles started happening behind the scenes and many warriors died to the buildup to the duel. Mind-games were played and Musashi went into hiding to create uncertainty with his enemies. On the day of the duel, Musashi arrived 4 hours late to confuse and unnerve his opponent. He then went on to defeat him.

At another duel, Musashi arrived 3 hours early and waited and saw an ambush being planned for him. Musashi jumped out defeated his opponent and disappeared.

At the very core of Budō is the idea that you never retreat and never give up. This means the heart of Budō is courage. This means whatever the obstacle keep moving forward and persevere.

In Japanese, "Do" means the way. "Bu" means military or war. Loosely Budō can be translated as martial way or way of the warrior.

In essence its a way of living life as a warrior.

So Why am I Talking To You About Budō?

Like I mentioned earlier Budō is an approach to life. Its a mindset of the warrior. Sure I get it we are not doing duels every day or meeting someone for a street-fight. However, we walk through life in the mindset that we are doing battle every day and should be ready for whatever the universe throws our way. Practically every day in our lives we walk through the streets we look at the world the way a warrior would. We actively observe and try to be aware and vigilant. We are always ready because we understand the reality of this planet and the uncertainty that comes with it.

Does this mean we walk around with a paranoid angry attitude? No of course not. Do we walk around looking like we are at war? No, of course not. However, we are awake, aware and vigilant. We remain on guard and ready to fight in the physical or mental sense. We know in the real world with all its battles there are no rules and that only victims think the world is an innocent place. So we practice a philosophy where we made the conscious choice not to be a victim nor wait for others to help us when chaos breaks out. We take responsibility for everything. Its a form of extreme personal responsibility. It goes above and beyond normal personal responsibility and owning what we do. It means that I take ownership of not just my actions but for who I am and my own existence.

All aspects of your life get approached with the mindset of small battles happening everywhere. Battles happening at work, at home, and within your own mind. At the heart of it, you don't back down. Every battle in life you confront, evaluate and then deal with it with courage. You never back down. In this process, you observe your own actions and weaknesses and try to improve on them consistently.

Why Adopt Budō in Your Life?

By taking in life in a more direct manner will give you a deeper understanding of life. You will also get a greater understanding into yourself and your own perceived limits and how you can overcome them. By living with a Budō code teaches you at a subconscious level to claw with your fingernails with an absolute relentless attitude towards life. You will develop a spirit of never giving up and learn to run towards adversity with courage. You will become the type of person that fights until his very last breath. Self-improvement is an always present and inseparable element of Budō philosophy. Budō is consistent personal development of the character and behavior.

In Japan, they say that Budō is the way of the Buddha. This way leads you to discover your true nature and wakes you up from the trance you have been in for most of your life. You break loose from the shackles of your own ego and start walking around like the giant you truly are.

The Budō Code Has Eight virtues

-Righteousness
    -Heroic Courage
    -Benevolence/Compassion
    -Respect
    -Honesty
    -Honor
    -Duty and Loyalty
    -Self Control

Martial Arts As a Vehicle For Personal Development

If you are not a Martial Artist I want to encourage you to consider learning a martial that is both practical and challenging. There is no point in studying a martial art that is not practical in the modern world. I have a lot of respect for traditional martial arts but I do think in the modern world some martial arts are more suitable for the society we live in today where sword fighting is limited. However, I do think to prepare yourself for defense against weapons is a good idea. This book is not focused on martial arts so I will give you my recommendations and a few options to consider. Its then up to you to do some research and make a choice on what martial art is a good fit for you.

There is no better tool than a martial art for all-round human development. It will challenge you and expose your physical and mental weaknesses. It will then put you in the position to either face those weaknesses or retreat. If you decide to live the Budō approach to life then you will confront those weaknesses both on and off the mat. You will attack life directly. You will stop hiding from life and start living with spirit and courage.

Gracie Jiujitsu

My martial art of choice is Gracie Jiujitsu or the more common name Brazilian Jiujitsu(BJJ). The term Brazilian Jiujitsu is a broad term for the more sports orientated form of JiuJitsu. However, Gracie Jiujitsu is a more traditional form of the same art and has its primary focus on the self-defense aspect of the martial art. Gracie Jiujitsu will teach you how to defend yourself and put you on a path of personal development. The Gracie Academy would be my recommendation if you choose to start training Jiujitsu. Unfortunately most modern Jiujitsu academies these days just focus on sport and therefore loses the heart of what Jiujitsu is all about.

The next part of this chapter will be a more detailed look into Jiujitsu so you have a better understanding of Jiujitstu. However, if you choose a different route then that is fine. There are many martial arts out there that are great to develop you as a human. Martial arts like Judo, Karate, Muay Thai are also great Self Defense systems.

Jiu Jitsu (BJJ)

The world at large didn't know anything about Brazilian JiuJitsu before Royce Gracie and the first four Ultimate Fighting Championship tournaments. Nevertheless, the core concept of the UFC tournament was shared by the founders of this martial art. Brazilian JiuJitsu (or BJJ) was catapulted to fame when the skinny Gracie won the first, second, as well as the fourth UFC tournaments fighting like a human anaconda that even relatively larger men feared.

Type of Art

BJJ is at its core a grappling martial art. It is a full-contact sport and competitions do not usually employ the usual safety gear such as helmets, shin guards, soft body armor, or even gloves. Although BJJ practitioners taking part in mixed martial arts do wear gloves, those who compete in pure BJJ competitions do not wear them.

The emphasis of this martial art is basically fighting on the ground. Studies show that the majority of all one on one hand to hand combats usually end up on the ground. Some estimate it from 60 to 80 percent of any street fight or aggressive encounter.

This is basically where Brazilian JiuJitsu shines where other traditional martial arts rarely put any emphasis. On the ground strength, size, and reach are rendered ineffective. Both the larger and smaller combatants are on equal footing when the fight is moved to the ground.

History

Brazilian JiuJitsu is popularly attributed to the Gracie family. However, it was Mitsuyo Maeda who brought the original martial art from Japan to the shores of Brazil. Maeda traveled the world to spread JiuJitsu and more so Judo. He slowly perfected his craft as he pitted his skills against practitioners of other martial arts.

Some of the skilled opponents that Maeda fought against included practitioners of savate, wrestlers, and even boxers. He arrived in Brazil on 14th of November 1914. While in Brazil, Maeda demonstrated his art to the local folks via the Queirolo Brothers' circus. This was where Carlos Gracie would first catch a glimpse of this martial art and fall in love with it forever.

Carlos studied Judo under the direct tutelage of Maeda. He learned this martial art for several years. He also passed his knowledge along to his brothers. Carlos' brother Helio slowly developed Brazilian Jiu Jitsu from the craft taught to him by his brother.

He had to adapt the martial art to his situation – he could not execute some of the moves employed in Judo, especially the ones that required one to oppose the strength of an opponent. His adaptations focused more on ground fighting. It basically turned the art into a form that is practical even for a smaller or weaker fighter.

Note that the Gracies are not the only originators of Brazilian Jiu Jitsu. Maeda had other students. One of them was Luiz Franca and is represented today by his students beginning with Oswaldo Fadda. The popular Brazil-based mixed martial arts team Nova Uniao, where dominant champions like Jose Aldo hail from, lean toward Fadda's BJJ style, which dominantly focuses on foot locks.

Strong Points

The strong points of this martial art are in its ground fighting. The fight is neutralized for both combatants, and the encounter is transformed as it were into a mechanical chess game on the floor. The more knowledgeable fighter fighting on his back eventually wins despite the lack of size or strength.

There are a lot of maneuvers that can be used by the disadvantaged combatant. Since a fight will most likely end up on the ground, a smaller or weaker opponent should expect to end up on his back eventually. If you don't know how to defend yourself while lying on your back, then expect the fight to end in a few moments.

However, this is where Brazilian JiuJitsu turns things around. Even if you are the weaker opponent, you can still take advantage of your position and attack even when your opponent is right on top of you. There are many ways you can strangle, lock, neutralize, and even break your opponent even if you are on your back. The philosophy is that when the fight moves into the ground phase, then both opponents are on equal footing. This is where knowledge of ground fighting comes into prominence in real life combat.

Practicality

There are a lot of practical applications of Brazilian JiuJitsu. It is very easy for anyone to admit that there is always someone who is stronger and bigger than you are. So, basing your martial arts skill on pure strength and size is in itself a self-defeating endeavor.In a street situation, BJJ is very practical and efficient.For people with limited physical strength, this martial art is a great fit.

Weaknesses

One of the fundamental flaws of Brazilian Jiu Jitsu is its entire lack of striking skills. Even though BJJ is demonstrably effective against traditional stand-up fighting techniques, there are ways to counter the attempts of a BJJ practitioner to take his opponent down to the ground.

Experience shows that a purely BJJ-based fighter or a purely stand up based fighter or striker can be outmatched by a well-rounded mixed martial artist. BJJ in the end requires something to balance its pure ground game, and that can come from other effective stand up fighting arts mentioned in this book.

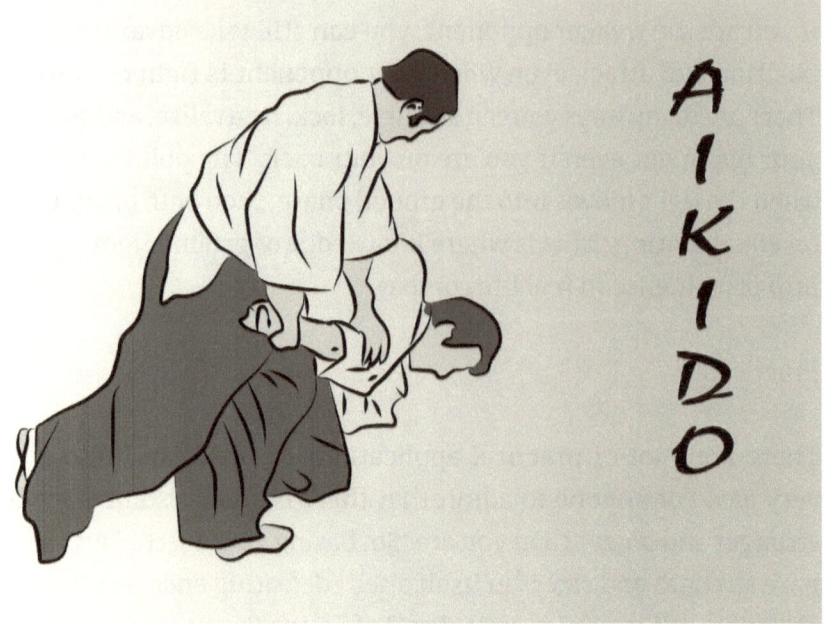

Aikido

You may have first seen the art of Aikido demonstrated in one of Steven Seagal's movies. It may have been quite an impressive thing to see him defeat five or more opponents with just a few simple strokes of his hands. He even defeats them in stunning fashion – some get thrown, others get broken limbs, and a few getting mortally wounded.

You may even recognize some of the throws and moves as a form of Judo or Jujutsu. Aikido was derived from these martial arts, which are its ancestors. After admitting that fact, an Aikidoka (Aikido practitioner) will also quickly add that his art is a lot smoother compared to the former arts.

Type of Art

Most will classify Aikido as a form of grappling art. Its main emphasis is in throws, pretty much like Judo, but it also has an equal emphasis on joint locks. Another signature of this martial art is the use of the opponent's momentum and not your strength. This is achieved using techniques in turning as well as entering thus diverting the direction of the opponent's force and neutralizing an attack.

History

The art of Aikido was created by Morihei Ueshiba. Just like other traditional martial arts from nation of Japan, this one also reflects the philosophy and religious views of its maker. The name Aikido simply means "The Way of Unifying the Life Energy."

The meaning behind the name of this combat system describes the overall approach it takes to win combat. And that is to blend your opponent's strength with that of yours and use both to win in combat. With that philosophy in mind, the Aikidoka will only need to use a small amount of his own strength to defeat his opponent.

Ueshiba developed his combat art and system in the period of 1920 to 1930. He synthesized the martial arts that he learned at the time into one system. At the very core of this martial art is Daitō-ryū aiki-jūjutsu, which Ueshiba studied directly under the hands of the famed Takeda Sōkaku.

In 1901 Ueshiba is also known to have studied under the renowned master of Tenjin Shin'yō-ryū by the name of Tozawa Tokusaburō. From 1903 to 1908, he was under the tutelage of Nakai Masakatsu as he studied Gotōha Yagyū Shingan-ryū. And in 1911 he learned Judo under Kiyoichi Takagi.

These martial arts have similarities as well as differences in principle, style, and approach. Nevertheless, Ueshiba leans towards Daitō-ryū as he developed the system which he will later call Aikido. Note that Ueshiba didn't merely focus on empty handed or barehanded combat methods. In fact, a huge section of his instructions dealt in the use of weapons particularly the sword.

The actual date when Ueshiba introduced Aikido is unknown, unfortunately. However, it is also known that he used to call this fighting system as Aiki Budo. The earliest usage of the name "Aikido" as an official name of this fighting system is in the year 1942.

Aikido spread throughout the world beginning in 1951 in France. In 1953 a martial arts tour was conducted in the United States. In that tour, Kenji Tomiki had the opportunity to demonstrate aikido in 15 US states. It was presented along with other prominent martial arts at the time.

However, it was Koichi Tohei who set up the first dojos in the United States in the islands of Hawaii. This was the first formal introduction of this combat art in the US.

Other practitioners and masters of the art were sent as official representatives and delegates of this art to different countries of the world. Nevertheless, the largest Aikido organization in the world is still the Aikikai Foundation, which is primarily run by the Ueshiba family. It should be noted that just like other martial arts, there are also variants and styles within Aikido. You may encounter one school that teaches one particular style which is different from what is taught in another – nevertheless, they all follow the same fundamental techniques and principles.

Strong Points

The strength of Aikido is in its focus in using your enemy's strength against him. The techniques used in Aikido resemble judo in certain aspects. An Aikidoka doesn't need to be the strongest warrior. He or she only needs to be the one who can better channel an opponent's force.

Techniques and moves in Aikido especially in self-defense can be used and mastered even by those who are obviously weaker and smaller. There aren't that many known tournaments in Aikido (except of course the few conducted by Shodokan Aikido) due to the fact that the moves, locks, throws, and breaks of aikido can be lethal.

Practicality

Aikido is a great option for smaller or weaker practitioners. You will basically rely in your knowledge of using your opponent's momentum against him. It is also a good option for those who are faced with multiple opponents.

Weaknesses

Aikido has been criticized with regard to the counter-maneuvers it presents. Some say that the attacks made by strikers including punches, kicks, and armed strikes are easy to deflect. Critics go on to say that if the supposed attacks practiced in the dojo are flimsy then the student will not understand how to defend himself in real life combat.

This critique is heavily debated. Those from the Shodokan Aikido school have demonstrated that aikido can be used in actual combat and in competitive format as well. However, there are sectors within the Aikido organization who are against competitive formats saying that it departs from the spirit of this combat art since it is not only a martial art or game, but a spiritual philosophy as well.

Muay Thai

Muay Thai is a martial art that hails from Thailand. Some people compare this combat art form to kickboxing, but there definitely are differences in both disciplines. Muay Thai at its core is both a physical as well as a mental discipline. It has become one of the more popular martial arts today.

Type of Art

This is one of the martial arts in this book that primarily focuses on a stand-up game. It's a striking art and some people may call it boxing mixed with a kicks and knees. However, another huge aspect of this martial art is clinch-fighting. Practitioners make use of the clinch to inflict powerful critical strikes against an opponent. That includes attacks using one's elbows using efficient angles to inflict more damage. In effect, it is not merely a distance striking art – it is also a form of close quarter combat.

History

Muay Thai has a long history that spans hundreds of years into the Thailand's past. It was initially a bare fisted fighting system used in ancient warfare. It eventually evolved as a type of competition among practitioners during local festivals that are usually held in temples. This fighting art became the main component of the fighting style used in the year 1560 under the reign of then King Naresuan.

The golden age of Muay Thai came along in 1868 under the reign of Rama V. This time, the king himself was interested in this combat art. Muay Thai started to be seen as a form of exercise as well as a type of martial art.

Starting in 1935 competition rules were established. The very first boxing rings for Muay Thai were established during this time. Referees were then included as a third man on the ring, just like in the case of boxing. The entire match was also divided into several periods also known as rounds.

The traditional hemp rope that was wrapped around the hands of fighters was replaced by boxing gloves. Later on, groin protectors, as well as coverlets made of cotton on the fighter's feet, were also added into the protective gear used in matches.

Muay Thai today has become a very popular sport all over the world. In fact, it is a staple in many mixed martial arts tournaments. It has been demonstrated to be effective against many classical striking arts including Taekwondo and Karate.

Strong points

A fighter will not only rely on his hands or feet when using Muay Thai. Kicks with knees and punches with elbows are effective tools to inflict the most amount of damage on an opponent. This is also why they call this fighting style as the Art of Eight Limbs. Your hands or feet can get hurt or damaged when used to strike against an opponent, but that won't stop a nak muay (i.e. a Muay Thai practitioner). The elbows, as well as the knees, are just as effective. Other than that, you can also use clinch fighting and defeat your opponent in close range.

A Muay Thai practitioner can employ pretty unconventional strikes compared to boxing and other pure fist striking sports and martial arts. Everyone is familiar with a jab, cross, and a hook. You may have even seen these punches thrown in odd angles.

However, a spinning back fist, cobra punch, or even a wild swing may come from an angle not familiar to most people. Elbow strikes such as horizontal, slash, reverse, uppercut, mid-air elbow strikes, spinning elbows, and horizontal elbow strikes will come as a surprise to any opponent, especially in a clinch situation.

Knees are also effective especially when in the clinch. Knee strikes include horizontal knee strikes, diagonal, straight, flying knee, curving knee strike, knee bomb, and step up knee strikes. They are also effective in close range and clinch fights.

Another strong point of Muay Thai is clinch-fighting. Some of the clinches used in this martial art include the swan neck, arm clinch, low clinch, and the side clinch. Once a clinch has been applied to an opponent, elbows and knees can be effectively used to inflict a lot of damage.

Practicality

Many of the strikes employed in Muay Thai can be executed by anyone with enough practice. This art can serve as an effective form of self-defense if you don't have any available weapons. Practitioners can also use this martial art to defend against multiple opponents.

Weaknesses

The drawbacks of Muay Thai are pretty much similar to any stand-up fighting system. Once the phase of the combat goes to the ground, then the Muay Thai practitioner will have no solid training or background in counterattacking a well-versed ground fighter. It should be repeated here that a huge percentage of all combat encounters eventually end up on as a match on the ground.

A Muay Thai practitioner, on the other hand, can cope with grapplers by applying take down defenses, which includes sprawling and maintaining a balanced stand-up position. This means that a practitioner of this art should incorporate a bit of ground defense in order to negate any attempts of an opponent to bring the fight on the ground.

Another downside of Muay Thai is that it has very little support for smaller and weaker fighters. This fighting system favors those who can strike harder and faster. Another issue is that a fighter that has a longer reach can have a significant advantage. A younger and stronger Muay Thai fighter has a significant advantage over a weaker opponent.

Judo

The name Judo literally means the "way of gentleness" or "the gentle way." But if you consider the techniques employed by this martial art, the general public would think that there is nothing gentle about it. It is a popular martial art and sport that eventually became part of the Olympics since the year 1964.

The art of Judo has taken the spotlight once again in the world of mixed martial arts. Some of the competitors in this newly developed sport have a Judo background. One of the most successful Judoka (Judo practitioner) of late is Ronda Rousey

Rousey won the Ultimate Fighting Championship's Women's Bantamweight belt; successfully defeating almost every opponent on the ground and with a signature finish – an armbar. Other popular figures in the world of Judo include Hector Lombard, Kayla Harrison, Fedor Emelianenko, Jimmy Pedro (instructor at the Olympic Training Center in Massachusetts), Hidehiko Yoshida, Yoshihiro Akiyama, and Vladimir Putin.

Type of Art

Even though Judo is basically a grappling art, its emphasis is in throws. In competitions, a match can be ended by executing a throw, or it can be finished via a grappling match on the ground. But throws and takedowns are the art's most prominent features.

On the ground, pinning techniques can be applied by a Judo practitioner to either subdue or at least immobilize an opponent. Joint locks, as well as chokes, are utilized in this martial art as well.

Some may not immediately agree that this combat art is entirely a ground fighting system since a lot of the techniques primarily focus on the stand-up phase and the takedown phase of an actual combat. However, striking and weapons defense are an integral part of the art. Students are actually taught how to use the principles of Judo as a self-defense in real life situations including threats from an armed opponent.

History

Judo was created by Jigoro Kano, who was also an educator. He studied jujutsu under different masters or teachers which included Fukuda Hachinosuke, Iso Masatomo, Iikubo Tsunetoshi. Each sensei (teacher) focused on different aspects of the art of jujutsu that included randori (freestyle practice), kata (pre-arranged combat forms), and nage-waza (throwing techniques).

Kano founded his own school in 1882. His teachings are both philosophical as well as combat oriented. He emphasized the achievement of maximum efficiency with the use of minimal effort. He also emphasized mutual benefit in combat where both parties in the fight learn from one another. One of his foremost teachings is that gentleness controls hardness.

Competitions were an integral part of Jujutsu and Judo. Even Jigoro Kano became a competition chairperson as early as 1899. Committees were made to create contest rules to regulate matches. Rules continued to be added in later years.

In 1930, the first All Japan Judo Championship was held. The World Judo Championships were first held in 1956. The first ever Women's

Championships were organized in the year 1980. Judo was first incorporated into the Olympics in 1964 and the first women's Judo event in the Olympics was held in 1988.

Strong Points

The strength of Judo is in its takedowns and ground game. Locks and chokeholds follow after putting the enemy effectively on the ground. If you want to solidify your takedown skills, then the best way to do it is to learn from one of the best Judokas in the business.

It is not primarily a striking art (i.e. punching and kicking) although it does incorporate some of the strikes in the kata. If faced with an opponent that has no background against a grappler, a Judoka can immediately gain the upper hand. A Judoka doesn't have to be the stronger, larger, or faster opponent to prevail in a match.

This aspect of this martial art was demonstrated even when Judo was pitted against its predecessor art of Jujutsu. This is one of the reasons why Judo was adopted as the national martial art of Japan in the 1800s. A demonstration of Judo against other combat art forms also convinced law enforcement officers in the country to make it as the martial art used by police officers and even in the military.

Practicality

One of the strengths of Judo is in its thrust or emphasis in the application of its techniques in realistic combat situations. Jigoro Kano highly favors the use of randori, or free form practice, although he too practices kata. This type of practice exposes a Judoka to situations that are not usually experienced during competition or a match in a dojo. In that aspect, Judo has the potential to evolve and transform into a broader art.

The techniques used in Judo can be used by older folks and even young children. Some of the techniques may require one to oppose the strength or momentum of an opponent, but many of aspects of the art practically makes use of your opponent's force, weight, and strength against him.

Weaknesses

One of the bigger drawbacks of Judo is pretty much the same with any grappling form of art. It's reduced emphasis on striking presents a particular weakness in the art. It tries to compensate for this lack by teaching students how to defend against strikers. However, it should be noted that a striker who has a pretty good takedown defense can prevent any attacks by a Judoka and make use his superior striking skills to take advantage of a combat situation.

10

Managing Ourselves

The key to Self Discipline that leads to a very high level of success is managing your time and personal productivity. In order for you to use self-discipline that leads to success, you need 2 elements to get you there. The first part is you feeling happy and content internally. And the second part is you effectively and relentlessly executing on your goals.

These 2 elements are like yin and yang to each other. They keep each other in balance and can't exist without each other. Think about this reality for a second. If you feel happy and positive inside but you don't have a mission and purpose in life then you will feel incomplete and slowly but surely your happiness will disappear.

On the other hand, if you have goals and a mission in life but you feel empty and negative on the inside then your goals and mission will start falling apart and become meaningless. Everything in the universe works in this type of yin and yang balance. You can't have hot without cold and hard without soft. This is the nature of the universe. This is also the nature of success.

So how do we make sure we stay happy but also stay very productive?

You Need To Create Your Startup Ritual

What is a startup ritual? A startup ritual is my list of actions I take every morning to start my day. Rituals or habits are very powerful.I already illustrated the power of habits in a previous chapter. I shared with you the story of Micheal Phelps the Olympic champion and how he used success habits and rituals to train his brain to become successful.

This startup ritual works very well because it sets the tone for the rest of the day. Once you execute your startup ritual the rest of the day gets so much easier. Your startup ritual makes you hit the ground running and makes the rest of the day so much easier.

So what should you include in your morning startup ritual? To create your ritual think about all the things that would empower you mentally, emotionally and physically?

Let's start by setting your alarm clock for 5:30 am. You want to be done with your ritual at 7 am. So you have an hour and a half for your startup ritual.

You can put whatever worked for you in your ritual. But I will share with you my ritual to give you an idea of how this works:

-Alarm Rings at 5:30. I get up to wash my face and brush my teeth.
   -Drink a Glass of Cold Water
   -Make a cup Of Coffee
   -Sit Down Read My Vision and Goals
   -Write Down My Goals On A piece of Paper
   -Finish my coffee and go sit down in a comfortable position
   -Visualize my vision

- Zazen Meditation
- Yoga
- After Yoga I Make a Berry Protein shake for breakfast.
- Take A Shower
- Start the Day

Be very specific about your ritual. For example what type of shake will it be? Will it be organic with green powder. Be very specific and tailor make your ritual to empower you. If you design your ritual into a powerhouse then you will be unstoppable the rest of the day. Unfortunately, most people start their day in chaos and the rest of the day they are just reacting and putting out fires. But if you have a startup ritual you will feel in total control of your day. The whole idea is to start your day with a lot of positive momentum.

Alignment

To create maximum productivity in your life you need to align everything in your life so its all focused on your mission. To illustrate this point lets look at the following example. Let's say a guy wants to be an Olympic Swimmer. So the guy starts swimming every week and going to the gym. But he also has a drinking habit twice a week. Those 2 nights he parties and drinks a lot of alcohol. He enjoys his time with friends. He fails in his goal because he is not aligned with his mission.

To reach your goals and achieve your vision for your life you need to align all the parts of your life. You can't say you want to achieve something great but parts of you are not aligned with that goal.

Go sit down and make 2 lists. The first list is your most important goals. Your second list is the things you spent the most time on. If the second list is not matching your goals then you are out of alignment. You need to be hard on yourself if you want to reach your goals. There are no compromises in this game.

Work In Single Focus Blocks Of 60 Minutes

Human focus has two parts. The first part is the quantity and the second part is quality. When you combine these 2 parts you get powerful results. So let's start with the quality and quantity part of the focus.

The quantity is the time you spent doing something. The quality is the thing that you choose to do within that time. This might seem obvious to many but there is big power with the right combination of both quantity and quality.

Let's start with time. You need to set a single block of time for your work of 60 minutes. The key is that this is an uninterrupted time.No smartphone, phone calls or any other distraction. We live in a time with a lot of distractions and most people have minds that are out of control. They cannot focus one thing for longer than 5 minutes. This is a problem and if you struggle to focus then start with a thirty-minute block of work and then build that focus up to an hour. After an hour take a 20 min break relaxing.

Don't surf the net or check your phone. Go for a walk or take a short nap. Then make a cup of coffee and start with your next 60 min block of time. Try and build up those 60 min blocks. If you struggle with focus then try and do 3 blocks and build it up to 6 blocks. Do whatever it takes to build up those blocks of focus.

The second part of building this focus muscle is to decide what it is you will focus on. In other words the quality part of your focus. A lot of people do a lot of "work" but don't accomplish much because they spend their time on the wrong things. You need to go sit down and make a list of the most important things in your life. Think about the things that will give you the most leverage over the next 5 years and longer. For example, physical training every day will give you long term health benefits. Working on creating content for your business will grow your company and make you money. Then break it down further. For example, weight training will give the most benefits so that is one block of time. Building my website will make me a lot of money so that is another block of time.

So you have to objectively look at your life and ask yourself what is the most important work you will focus on? This will be the quality part of your focus.

Time

Time is your most important commodity. Once it's gone you will never get it back. So use it wisely and start looking at how you spend your time. You have to manage your time efficiently. Plan everything. This means your days, weeks and hours. You have to become very deliberate in the way you live.

You need to observe you days, weeks and months to figure out where you are wasting time. Start writing down how many hours you sleep and manage it accordingly. You don't need or more than 6 hours of sleep a night.

Organization

You need to manage your house, car, office, computer, email, social media so that you are in control. Don't allow these variables to control you. You have the power to control these things. It's up to you to create order in them. You have to be organized in all these areas or they will affect everything else you do. Keep everything clean, crisp and in its place.

Goals and Vision

In life, you need a vision. This means you need to know where you are going otherwise you are on the road to nowhere. If you don't have a vision for your life its like driving a car without a map. You are just driving without really going anywhere.

After you have set up your vision you need to set up your goals. Break those big goals down into monthly goals so that you can track your progress. Go over your goals every morning before work and every night before you go to sleep. Best way to do this is to write it down every day on a blank piece of paper. This way these goals get driven deep into your subconscious mind so you constantly feel the need to take action on them.

Executing Consistently

You need to become a relentless executing machine. Take the massive action towards your goals and vision. Stay focused and stay the course. Don't take your eye off your goals. Follow your plan and don't let anyone get you off your path and your mission. The resistance will come to try and stop you. People will try and stop you. Your emotions will try and stop you, failures will try and stop you, your mind will try and stop you. But above it all, you must rise up like a king and dominate. Dominate like a warrior armed with the great big sword of Self Discipline.

Preparation

Make sure you are ready for every day by being prepared. Make sure your alarm clock is set for the next day. Get your bags packed and clothes ready to put on. Prepare your breakfast and set it up for an easy exit. You need to hit the ground running. Remember, "Victory loves preparation."

Taking Time out

On Sundays take a day off to rest and reflect. Most importantly take 20 min and practice some gratitude. This might sound a bit corny but its necessary to stay grounded and focused. Be grateful for what you have achieved so far but also recognize that you can do a lot more. Spend the day relaxing and spending time with your loved ones like your girlfriend/wife/family/kids.

11

Finding Focus

The world will resist your efforts. You need to build a mindset based on an incredibly strong focus. Your vision should be in your mind constantly and at the same time, you need to let it go by focusing on long term goals and monthly goals. This will drive you. The focus will be your superpower.

You need to funnel everything you do every day into this funnel of discipline.Meditation ,exercise,diet,sacrifice etc.It all funnels into your self Disciplined focus. It all comes together in this machine of focus. Your focus is building on your Self Discipline.

All your daily actions and choices are building your culture of control and self-discipline. Your mindset is where you bring it all together. You know that Self Discipline is the tool to live a life of success and abundance.

The way you think about daily life is going to be massively important.

The Power Of Positive thinking

Don't worry I'm not telling you to blindly think the world is always a nice place because we all know that is not true. What I am telling you is that positivity has incredible power to drive you forward and push closer to your vision. Staying Disciplined every day, every week and every year can become draining if you don't frame it all in a positive light. Yea I get it, a lot of bad stuff happens, but we all have a choice every day. A choice to see the positive or the negative. We choose what we focus on.

A lot of people quit Self-discipline and with that goes all their dreams and goals. One of the big reasons for this is that they focus on the negative side of their experiences. They could have focused on the positive but the negative was so tempting that they gave into it. The truth about negativity is that there is such an abundance of it that you never have a hard time to find a lot of it. It's everywhere you go. Negativity on the news, social media, gossip etc.It 95% negative.

For example, you go to the gym and you get tortured by your personal trainer. You hurt and for the next few days, you are in pain.A little voice starts telling you "That trainer is too harsh" "I don't need this in my life. Or your friends start saying things like "We like the old you better" or "Why do you want to do Weight training?"So all these negative thoughts, statements, and emotions are suddenly in abundance. Most people give in to them. But what if you changed the frame to the positive? What if you listened to the positive voice?The one that says" If I keep this up I will lose all this fat and look great" or "If I get through this pain I will get the body I want and get my confidence back."What if you focused on this positive voice? Well, the answer is simple. You won't quit. You will keep on going. You will accept the pain and keep your discipline.

What you focus on is a choice. You will have to make these little choices daily and consistently. The easiest way to get through them is to focus on the positive frame.

Build a Ritual Of Focus

By now you should have written out your vision for your life and all your goals. Every morning when you wake up and take a shower. Then make a cup of coffee. Go sit down and take out your journal with your vision and goals. While sipping on your coffee start reading your vision out loud to yourself. Do this 3 times.

After you finished reading your vision take a look at your goals. Do the same thing. Read your goals out loud for yourself. Then take a pen and write out your goals 3 times on a piece of paper. The exercise of writing your goals down every morning will cement them in your mind.

Now finish your coffee and go sit a or lie down in a comfortable place. Put on some nice relaxing music. It has to be relaxing music with no words to put you in a trance. Now close your eyes. Start visualizing your vision of your life and see yourself already achieving all those things in your life vision. Take 10 minutes for this part of the exercise. Then visualize for another 10 minutes how you successfully achieve all your goals. For example, if you want to climb Mount Everest. See yourself at the top of the summit smiling and then safely going down. Feel the cold air on your face and the sun in your eyes. Use all your senses and let the music take you away and stir your creativity. Don't think this is some pointless exercise. Visualization is one of the most powerful exercises you can do.

Like I mentioned in a previous chapter Elite Special Forces and elite Athletes use visualization to train their minds to stay disciplined and reach their objectives. The mind can not differentiate between the pictures in your mind and reality. By doing this you are training your subconscious mind to get in the habit of being successful.

Only Think About The Next 5 Minutes

A lot of people are not successful because they get overwhelmed by the big picture. They think about the massive task in front of them and they freeze. Elite athletes like Micheal Jordan says that he used to only focus on the next play, he never thought about what was at stake. He said that if players started thinking about winning championships their focus wasn't in the game. So whenever you are starting something new or taking a new direction in life don't get overwhelmed and turn it into this big thing in your mind. All you have to do is think about the next 5 minutes and then the next 5 minute after that.

Special Operations candidates have to go through the brutal selection and training courses to eventually qualify as a Special Operations Operator. For example, a Green Beret Special Forces candidate has to go through the Special Forces Selection course, the Qualification Course, language school, survival school, airborne school and some go through Ranger School. This takes up to 2 years or even more. Almost 70% of candidates don't make it through the 2 year period.

At the beginning of this period, candidates can get overwhelmed at the mountain that lies ahead and the reality of the odds against them. During this time the fear of the mental and physical mountain ahead make many candidates start doubting themselves. The candidates are taught to only focus on the next 5 minutes. The 5-minute rule will get you through situations that you thought was not possible by placing your focus in the now and the next 5 minutes.

Let Go Of Things You Can't Control

There are some things in life you can't control. It's natural for the human mind to start wondering and start thinking about things outside its reach. If something is out of your control then let it go. Don't make yourself sick with worry. If you start thinking about these things then stop. Bring your mind back to what you are doing right now and start thinking about the next 5 minutes.

Open Sets

In life, we start things and we don't finish them. Or we get ourselves into situations that we don't deal with. For example, you start writing a book but never finish it. Or you get into an argument with someone and never resolve the conflict. These are open sets in your mind. These open sets plague your mind and messes with your focus. You need to deal with these issues and resolve them. When you do this you will remove weight off your shoulders. For example, finish the book you were writing or go and talk to the person you are arguing with and resolve it. Done.

Focus On What You Want To Achieve In Life Not What You Want To Avoid

A lot people make the mistake taking actions to avoid a certain outcome. What they should be doing is just focusing on the positive outcome. The subconscious mind will start going towards a negative outcome if you focus on it. Think big and think about your ideal outcome. Your target is all that matters.

12

The Secret Of Sacrifice

A large part of Self Discipline is based on sacrifice. Sacrifice is a very important component of self-discipline. But its also the key to getting everything you want in life. Giving things up now so you can live your dream life.

Remember this. You can have anything you want in life but you can't have everything. You need to make some important choices and you will have to let some things go. You will have to let many things go so you can reach your goals in life and reach your full potential.

Some people never get what they want in life because they get seduced by choice. Choice is one of our greatest gifts. However within this gift is a hidden danger. This danger is not making a choice on what you will focus on. I see this all the time, guys want to make a change but they can't choose something they want to go after so they chase many targets at once. The problem is they never catch any of them and achieve nothing. For example, you can't say you want to start a business but also start studying a Masters degree in Science. You have to choose one and go after it with everything you got.

I asked you earlier in this book what is your "why"? Why do you want to be Self Disciplined? We all have reasons for bringing discipline into our lives. There is immense value in Self-Discipline just by itself. Just as a tool for survival on this planet. However, I know if you are reading this book you have giant goals you want to achieve and an even bigger vision for your future. Self Discipline will be the vehicle to get you those things. For you to get those things you need to make friends with sacrifice. More than friends, you need to embrace it.

How badly do you want to reach your goals? Is it just a something you dabble in? Or is it an absolute must for you? It's easy to talk and be the man at the parties. We all know that guy. The guy who is always talking about those great things he is going to do but he never takes any actions to achieve it. If you ask him about it a year later he will have some excuse to why he didn't do it. The reason why most of these men fail is that they are not willing to give it all up. They are not willing to sacrifice to get what they want. They are not willing to embrace their friend self-discipline. These men choose instant gratification over long term victories. These men are afraid of pain and run at the first sight of shadows. The big talkers show their true colors when you confront them and ask them about their results.

Sacrifice is the fuel you put into your car that takes you toward your vision. Every-time you sacrifice something for the greater good of your mission you put in more fuel and your engine runs stronger and more powerful. You start driving longer distances and drive all over the place in your car. This car is has a name. It's called success.

Next Level Discipline

The fact that you are reading this book means you mean business. You are serious about success and you want to reach your goals. You are not willing to sacrifice on that. Your obsession with your mission drives you to do whatever it takes to get what you want. You know that in order for you to win you need to study the masters.

You need to study the GOATS as they say in the NBA. The GOATS are the greatest of all time. If you think of GOATS in basketball you think of guys like Kobe and MJ.If you think about GOATS in business think of Elon Musk, Peter Thiel and Grant Cardone to name a few. There are GOATS in all fields. Whatever fields you are in you need to find the GOATS and study them? Read their biographies and find out as much as possible from them. Then ask yourself what can you learn to from them and implement in your own life?

Motivation is not enough

Like I mentioned earlier in this chapter motivation is not enough to get you there. You need to go sit down and figure out your reason for doing this. Then sit down and write it down on a piece of paper. Read it every morning when you get up and every night before you go to bed.

So What Do we need if Motivation Is Not Enough

I love motivation, it gives me that needed a boost every now and then I recommend you do the same. However, there is something else more powerful than just motivation. This thing has gotten a very bad reputation but its one of the most powerful things in the universe if you use it right.

This thing is an obsession. Are you obsessed with your mission? Are you obsessed with your purpose?

I don't understand the big generalization people make about being obsessed.I mean people are sometimes obsessed about things that do nothing for them or things that are very bad for them. Then people don't really give criticism for those things. For example, when someone is obsessed with some TV show which they obsessively watch then people joke about it and think its cool. If someone smokes a lot of cigarettes nobody stops that person and say "Hey I think you are a bit obsessed with that smoking thing".But as soon as someone works a lot and absolutely loses himself in his mission on this planet people have a problem with it. Suddenly people are concerned and say things like "You need more balance in your life".Or "you need to take a break".Another good one is "You are an obsessive work-person".Well, yes I am an obsessive work-person. I am obsessed with my success and potential. Why is that a bad thing?

Motivation is not something that keeps you up at night, but obsession does. It's something that is always in your mind. When you go to the gym, in the shower or going for a run its always there. Your purpose consumes you.

What are You Willing To Give Up To Get What You Want?

How obsessed are you with your mission and what are you willing to give up to get it. When you become so obsessed with your mission that it consumes you people will judge you. They will try to stop you. They don't understand that your drive comes from a deep and meaningful place. Your vision is so large that nothing less than total obsession will get you there. They don't understand that your "selfish "behavior is to accomplish your vision. And when your vision becomes a reality you will change the world. They won't understand it and don't expect them to understand it. You will realize that Self-Discipline and sacrifice can become a very lonely road. But you accept that. You know this in itself is the sacrifice. You have to be willing to do whatever it takes to reach your goals.

When I started implementing extreme self-discipline into my life I annoyed of a lot of people. I didn't do anything to other people, however, my obsession with my mission made them freak out. They resented my extreme focus and dedication. They started hating me for saying no to all the party invites and social gatherings. They started hating me for going to the gym when they were drinking. They got annoyed when I didn't show up for new years celebrations. They got annoyed with it all.

They didn't understand that I was willing to give it all up. I gave up my social life, alcohol, parties, junk food, hobbies and I even later moved to a different country to go after my goals. I was resented for everything. But that was what I was willing to sacrifice to get what I want.

My focus every day is on keeping my self-discipline. This discipline gives me the freedom to be obsessed with my vision and goals. I am 180% invested in myself. The irony about Self Discipline is that extreme levels of Self Discipline and sacrifice give you everything you ever wanted.
   The bottom line is this. Self-Discipline will set you free.

Like I mentioned earlier in the book ,you need to observe you days, weeks and months to figure out where you are wasting time. If something is not aligned with your mission. Then cut the cord and sacrifice it all.

Comfort Zones Will Be Your Enemy

When you first start making self-discipline part of your life you will see some improvements. However, the danger will be if you fall into the trap of the comfort zone. For example, earlier in my life, I made some improvements in my life and I got a job that was comfortable and the pay was decent. I made good money and I got comfortable. I got so much comfort that I got stuck. I was just getting my money and living out my days without making any real improvements. I thought I was good.

Before I knew it 4 years had passed and I was still in that job and had saved no money. I was spending, going on vacation and had been seduced by comfort. My self-discipline went out the door and got lost in the comfort zone. The thing about a comfort zone is that you don't see it coming.It sneaks up on you and before you know it you have drowned in the comfort. The lesson in this story is to never get too comfortable. When you get to a point where you feel like your "good" then take that as a signal that you are vulnerable. Don't get seduced by a little success or progress. Always make sure you are in control, working hard and pushing forward within your culture of Self Discipline. Be persistent and relentless in your efforts to reach your goals.

13

Mental Toughness

Mental Toughness is the process of maintaining Self Discipline. When the whole world expects you to quiet you don't. When the whole expects you drop your standards, you don't. When the world around you burn you still keep on marching forward. On the surface that is mental toughness.

But mental toughness is a lot deeper than that. It's just not one thing, its thousands of moments and little choices where you decide to keep going or quit.

Mental Toughness is a term that gets thrown around a lot these days. It's almost a cool thing to talk about. A lot of people make it sound like its something you can get like a commodity. But the truth is that mental toughness is not just something you acquire once and you're done. Its gets developed through backbreaking hard work. It gets forged in the deepest parts of your being. There in the deepest corners of your body, mind, and soul, your mental toughness gets sculpted. You sculpt it like an artist sculpts a statue. It's a process.

How does this process look?

How do you build mental toughness?

(1) You need to Go back and face your past

Now the first reaction from a lot of guys is "wait a minute John, what does my past have to do with my mental toughness and self Discipline?" My answer? "Everything".

I have mentioned before that everything is connected. When it comes to things like mental toughness and Self Discipline your past plays a massive role in your development.

So the next question is why is it important? Well, we all have a past and a story. That story we tell ourselves has played a massive role in our development, mindset, weaknesses, and strengths. It has influenced the way we see ourselves and what we believe is possible.

The truth of those things in our past is that they return to haunt us in the times when we should be at our best. These bad things that happened to us form bad mental habits. For example, maybe you had a big relationship disappointment like a bad breakup. That breakup made you stop believing in yourself and you started to tell yourself you are not good enough. Now a year later in a very challenging time in your business that wound still haunts you. Why? Because you never took time out to face it and deal with it and take responsibility for it.

Most people live life in denial and blame other people and we drag these things with us? The results are that we lose our confidence and self-belief. We need to confront our past so we don't drag it with us. When we are free from those things we get stronger, more confident and focused on our future.

After we face our past, we cut it lose and let it go. It's done, we learned from it and got stronger. We don't blame anyone for anything. We take full responsibility for our past and future.

(2)Observing The Choices We Make Every day

Life is a very long series of choices, Every choice you make has a domino effect. Every effect has a cause.

-What time do you get up?
  -What do you eat every day?
  -Do you exercise?
  -What do you eat?
  -Did you make the Sales calls?
  -Did you Go to JiuJitsu ?
  -Did You Approach that beautiful girl?
  -How many hours a day do you work?
  -How many hours do you sleep?
  -Do you drink when you know you shouldn't?
  -Did you watch TV last night?
  -How many hours were you on social media?
  -How many interruptions did you allow?

Every day these choices and questions come up. We must ask ourselves this question: **How consistently do we make the best choice?**

When you combine good choices with consistency you get a very powerful and effective combination. These small daily actions and evaluations over long periods of time make a large part of what mental toughness is all about. It's not flashy or glamorous but it had immense power.

Let's take exercise for example. An average person goes to the gym 2 or 3 times week. And when I talk about average I'm talking about the small group that actually goes. Within that group, the person will go 3 times then maybe takes some weeks off because there were some parties and work dinners. Then they will go again the next week twice but won't go the third time because their body is hurting from the last session.

Now let's look at the person with a high level of self-discipline combined with a well-developed level of mental toughness. This person will be in the gym 6 days a week every week for months and only take days of with serious injury or illness. They just keep on grinding. Things like hot or cold weather are irrelevant to them. There is only weather. They adapt improvise and keep on grinding. For the casual observer, it's just that one guy who always shows up. Always grinding. He is absolutely relentless in what he does.

Perseverance

I mentioned the world consistency earlier and consistency is very closely linked with perseverance but with a subtle difference. Perseverance can be defined as "steadfastness in doing something despite difficulty or delay in achieving success."This means that when you are absolutely physically exhausted and mentally drained you still push forward. You claw with your fingernails and drag yourself forward to get that next inch.You know that when you count up all those inches that it's going to make the difference in winning or losing. So you fight for every inch like its the last one on the planet. You always keep moving forward.

Perseverance is the heart of mental toughness because here is the bottom line: You don't have to do this. You can leave right now. You can stop reading this book or listening to the audio-book. You don't need this self-discipline.All the discomfort and pain. You don't need the early mornings and the late nights. You don't need the healthy food and all the missed holidays and parties. You can let it all stop right now. All you have to do is quit. Just tell yourself its over. Then its done. However, the mentally tough person will hear all these little voices in his head and he has heard them thousands of times when he is under pressure.But they don't have power over him anymore.He is now in control. He is now the master of his mind. Sure he goes through hard times but he perseveres he gets over obstacles because his purpose and vision for his life is strong he can't be stopped. He has cultivated mental toughness and an extreme level of self-discipline.

Small Wins

When you start thinking big and going after massive goals you will need to fight and overcome many obstacles. You will get tired and things might seem overwhelming at times. In times of battle think about the next small win. So let's say for example you have a goal of making $30000 a month with your online business.This might seem hard to achieve and that is why many people give up. But a good way to mentally overcome this obstacle is by focusing on getting small wins. For example selling your fist product. That is a small win. Selling your first 100 is a small win. Another example in Jiujitsu is getting your first stripe on your belt is a small win. Getting your second stripe another small win.When you start building these small wins you start creating massive wins.

Patience

In a world of instant gratification where people want things right now, many people live in a fantasy world. A lot of people give up because they lack patience. Patience is such a subtle thing that many people miss it. In my line of work with online businesses it is very common. For example, people see others making money online and they fall for the marketers selling them on the overnight success stories. Don't fall for this myth of overnight success. It does not exist. The truth is that any success takes time. Sure you can get there reasonably fast but don't expect to become a millionaire in a year. Think big but don't think anything of real value gets created overnight. Part of what mental toughness is about is to quietly go about your business while others are complaining on social media pages about "When will I start making money?".Stay away from these types of toxic mentalities and focus on your mission. Just stay relentless and keep on building your small wins until that stack of small wins turn into a mountain and you get your massive win.Stay hungry and stay patient.

The Shiny Object Syndrome

The shiny object syndrome is when people jump from one thing to another without settling on one thing and becoming good at it. The shiny object syndrome breaks many dreams into tiny pieces and many never recover from it. Personally, I wasted a year chasing after something stupid and then came back on my mission.I'm one of the lucky ones that only lost a year. Others lose a lot more than that and never recover.

The shiny object syndrome is very common in business and entrepreneurial circles. People jump around from one thing to another. For example, a person starts an online consulting business but then jumps into crypto-currencies because that is the "Next big thing".And with this specific example of crypto we now know a lot of people ended up disappointed. In order to avoid this mind virus, you need to be mentally disciplined and start saying no to a lot of things. Don't fall for these shiny objects. Stay focused and say No. Stay on your mission.

Criticism Is Part Of The Game

The more Self Discipline becomes part of your life the more success you will create. With that success will come criticism. This is part of the reality when you put yourself out there and make some moves. People you never heard off will have opinions about you. That is part of the reality when you become successful. Expect it to come and don't let it get you of your mission. Stay focused.

How Do You React To The World?

The world is going to come at you that it inevitable.The only question is how will you react when it does? Let's look at how you can respond when things don't exactly go your way.How can we control our reactions?

(1)Control your environment. If you know, you get angry when you stand in a line at the bank then change it by being proactive. Go early when there are no lines. So you have controlled the situation.

(2)Reframe your reality. If you feel disappointed because for example you cannot afford a trip to Spain for the summer, then reframe it by telling yourself that you can take a nice trip in your own country. It's not perfect, but you still got your holiday. You can reframe your reality.

(3)Change your focus. If you go to for a drive and compare your car with others and feel negative about your life. Start focusing on what you have compared to the people taking the bus.

(4)Change your response in situations. Everything begins with awareness. If you get angry when someone makes a joke about you, then become aware of this. Then next time it happens, take a couple of deep breaths and react differently. For example, smile and just laugh at the person.

(5)The important thing to remember is that we have a choice how we react in any situation. You have a split second before you react. Take a deep breathe and choose wisely.

Changing your mind is a process so be patient and keep working on it.

Blog: https://masculinemindset.com/

14

ENTREPRENEURSHIP INTRODUCTION

Good entrepreneurs are the artists of the modern world. They take ideas and create remarkable products and services. They can take an empty canvas and create things that seemed impossible.

Steve Jobs is probably one of the most talked about entrepreneurs of our time.He revolutionized the way we look at technology!He made browsing the internet an artistic experience.If you ever had an iPad or Apple product in your hand, then you would know what I mean. Apple products are special and unique. Now it's one of the biggest and cutting edge companies in the world. They made magic out of nothing.

The important thing to remember is that Apple started out as an idea in someone's bedroom.Steve Jobs was a normal guy and with the help of a couple of friends they started something remarkable that changed the world.

You have the same opportunity to create something remarkable. You can take your ideas and create your vision. Today people have more resources than any other time in history.The internet has made knowledge freely available and has created massive opportunities.

Sure, becoming an entrepreneur is not easy. There are risks involved.

The path might be filled with disappointments, but if you persevere and work hard, then success is yours for the taking.

The world is changing, and more brave people are taking the big step and becoming entrepreneurs. The traditional path of working for 30 years and retiring is becoming outdated.

If you are thinking of becoming an entrepreneur, then it means you are different, brave and willing to walk the path less traveled.

I hope you enjoy this book, and that it inspires and helps you to take the next step in becoming an entrepreneur.

Good Luck!

15

What is Entrepreneurship?

Entrepreneurship is the process of building a business venture from scratch. More than that, it is a way of life. The path of the entrepreneur has been taken by many famous individuals like Bill Gates, Elon Musk, Mark Zuckerberg, and Richard Branson among others. These people have brought significant contributions to the world, by creating new things and defying the status quo.

Entrepreneurship is a lifestyle combined with the passion of learning new things, creating answers to problems, leading people towards a positive goal, and giving value to the world. Many of today's advancements have been brought by entrepreneurs and innovative thinkers. These people who have dared to be different and took on a great amount of risk are the reasons why the world is a better place to live in.

Entrepreneurship as an Alternative Career Option

Still, not everything in the world is as perfect as many expect them to be. In several economies, the outlook is grim as there are fewer jobs offered to people. The opportunities for employment and gain become smaller each day. Instead of depending on big companies and corporate firms, you can start small and build your own enterprise.

Entrepreneurship is a great alternative which can give you fulfillment in seeing your prized idea come to life.

It seems that entrepreneurship is becoming more popular nowadays. More fresh graduates, for example, are starting their own food businesses instead of joining the ranks of corporate organizations. News and magazine interviews tell of younger individuals who eventually made millions from a business they started out as hobbies on top of their education. Of course, who can forget about those who have dropped out of school to pursue something bigger than a diploma? People like Steve Jobs have done this, and now he is considered a legend.

Entrepreneurship requires no age restriction. You can start even if you are in your late 30s, 40s, or 50s. Colonel Sanders of Kentucky Fried Chicken fame had the idea for his business when he was 65. The only requirement needed to pursue a business venture is the willingness to start.

The Benefits of Entrepreneurship to the Human Spirit

Once you become an entrepreneur, there is no going back to the office or being an employee of a big firm. You will now crave for freedom and creativity to run your own venture. Here are just some of the benefits that entrepreneurs get in being their own boss.

1. The Freedom to Follow One's Own Voice

Instead of following your boss' instructions, you become free to follow your own wishes. You can do anything you want. You have the power to work when you want to, and stop when you feel like it. Your ideas become of great importance as you embark in entrepreneurship to make your ambitions happen.

2. Control of One's Time and Flexibility

Time is the greatest treasure of all, not money. When you control your own time, you are controlling your own destiny. Unfortunately, employees do not have a say on how to manage this valuable resource. They have to be at the beck and call of their superiors, which is not exactly one of the best feelings in the world.

3. Excitement

Every day in the life of an entrepreneur is a challenge. No two days are the same. On some days, you will be earning a lot, and then the next few months could carry a dry spell. If you dislike routine, then you are going to like the career path of an entrepreneur for its variety and propensity for excitement.

4. Pride in Achieving Goals

As an entrepreneur, you dictate your own goals. You will acquire a sense of pride in accomplishing your dreams and making things happen. It would also be sweeter to achieve since you will pass through difficulties first before earning success.

5. A Chance to Learn New Things

You have the ability to learn things you are deeply interested in, as well as in topics you would rather skip. As an entrepreneur, you have to be well-rounded in knowing all the possibilities to aptly prepare for potential problems. Learning new knowledge will give you the edge needed in running the business.

6. Limitless Earnings

An employee would have a fixed salary, while entrepreneurs do not. Part of the sacrifices you have to make is to throw job security out the window. From now on, you don't have a limit to how much you earn. Every income you will get is a direct result of your efforts and a few strokes of luck.

7. Building Self Esteem

The more an entrepreneur builds a bigger and stronger enterprise, the more his confidence in himself grows. Entrepreneurs are also known as nicer bosses since they have a relatively kinder approach in handling stress.

8. The Opportunity to Get the Full Reward

The full reward may include huge income, media coverage, or simply the joy in living out your dreams and being successful at it. As an entrepreneur, you are entitled to the full rewards of your efforts since each day is a challenge well fought.

The Benefits of Entrepreneurship to the Community

The advantages of entrepreneurship do not end with the individuals who have taken the risk of establishing their own enterprise. Its benefits extend up to the community which they help as a result of their efforts.

1. Generating New Jobs

Small to medium enterprises help communities by providing jobs to the locals. Entrepreneurs become more engaged with the community they live in by making a direct impact in the lives of their people. In times of economic difficulties, entrepreneurs help people earn money by making use of their skills to achieve the goals of the business.

2. Creating an Impact to the Economy

Businesses drive the lifeblood of the economy. They stimulate activity and give value to the total domestic income of the country. There are more benefits as well when citizens decide to support local businesses. Incomes get higher, and people generally become happier.

3. Provide Solutions to Problems

Lastly, entrepreneurship provides answers. They create value which people pay for to solve their problems. This opportunity is a rare one which can only be started by creative minds keen on building their own business. If you want to make the world a better place, start by finding a problem which you can solve and exchange for value.

16

How To Become An Entrepreneur

Becoming an entrepreneur is a mixture of science and art. You need plans to form the logic part of the business. This includes setting up shop, offering a product or a service, and attaining business quotas to generate income. At the same time, running a business is an art form. You need to understand the inner workings of the mind of your customers to become profitable.

Identify a Niche

Before starting a business venture, settle on a niche which you will serve. Focus on that area and center your products and services based on what the niche requires. For example, you want to open a restaurant. Decide first what kind of food you will serve your customers. Will it be healthy dishes, seafood meals, fast-food fare, or dessert items?

Write a Business Plan

The business plan is one of the most important resources of an entrepreneur. The plan highlights your vision, your mission, the goals of your business, and the financial projections needed by the business to stay afloat. Investors also require seeing the business plan before they decide to lend you money for capital in starting up shop.

However, I want to contradict myself a bit here. A business plan is not everything. I have started several businesses without one. But in hindsight, a business plan does give you direction and a roadmap so you can follow your progress and make sure you are becoming successful.

Offer Value for a Product or Service

The nature of your business' existence lies in the products and services you will offer to your market. Don't just offer what people need or want, create value that will justify the price and the usability of your products and services. Better yet, invent of an edge that will make your business a more attractive choice over competitors.

Pinpoint a Target Market

Your niche screens the potential consumers of your products and services. If you are serving healthy options for lunch, then that means you are ruling out people looking for fried food items as potential customers. It's impossible to attract everybody because that will mean your business does not have a brand which to identify with. Focus on your primary markets and refine offerings to cater to the taste of your targets.

Do Research

Relying on gut feel is one thing. At some points in running your business, you will encounter occasions where you are forced to decide on the spot. On these events, using your instincts is wise and recommended. But for the other aspects of the business, you should rely on research and calculated guesses. Do research as to what kind of items or services your target market will like and probably pay for. Never assume. Base your decisions on the data you have collected in refining the offerings and price points of your business.

Build a Startup

The ultimate test that an entrepreneur will face includes building the startup business from the ground up. You, as the head of the business venture, will face several difficulties and losing streaks of luck before you reach the line of success. Consider your new startup as your own child. Treat it with care and attention, but be objective enough to acknowledge shortcomings. Be flexible in running operations yet remain firm in your decisions. Allow for space in making mistakes. Learn the ropes of steering the business in profitable directions. You will get to success eventually if you play your cards right.

Handle Your Finances

Handling money correctly is perhaps the most underrated advice entrepreneurs receive when asking for tips on how to successfully build a business. Never underestimate the power of money. Most businesses fail in the first few years because the managers practice incorrect ways in handling the cash flows. If you want your business to succeed, you have to know where each cent goes. Manage the cash flow well and prevent unnecessary expenses from eating up your business' capital.

Last Piece of Advice: Take a Stand

As mentioned, entrepreneurship is a lifestyle. It's beyond the path of having a career; it extends into your personal life as well. In this line of thought, be prepared to fight naysayers if you truly want to succeed. You will encounter many of them as you climb up and accomplish milestones in your chosen career.

A tip is to be persistent. Take a stand from unsupportive circles like skeptic family members and friends. Learn how to focus your efforts effectively and never take your eyes from the prize. Lastly, persevere and never give up. You will find that you are closer to success the greater your problems become, so just keep on going. You will get there eventually.

17

Entrepreneurship Success

Entrepreneurship is defined as a way of thinking, reasoning, and acting. This is according to Jeffrey Timmons, in his book New Venture Creation. It is more than just having the talent and skills, it needs to be properly and strategically planned, it also requires passion and discipline to build a business that will last and you will enjoy doing. That is just some of the characteristics an individual must have to attain entrepreneurship success.

An entrepreneur is an individual who operates, manages, and controls a business in having the goal to earn profit. And to reach his goals, he must have these traits and attitudes:

1. Be Passionate

Passion is an important ingredient to achieve success. This will take you to the highest of your potential to reach your goals.

Do your best and you will exceed your limits as an entrepreneur. And to do your best, you must love what you are doing. Having no passion for work will just result to laziness and procrastination. If that happens, you'll never complete or attain your goals.

2. Be Disciplined

You need to focus on your goals, so that you can accomplish things needed in your business. If not, you will need to make more time to repair the damages or spend more time to finish your products or services.

There may also be changes from time to time about the demands of your customers and your capacity to work with it. It can give you stress that's why you also need to be flexible. Whatever changes that might happen in your business, you must be able to cope up with it.

3. Be a Risk-taker

As an entrepreneur, you must risk a lot of things especially money in starting your business. You must forget your fears and face the opportunities with confidence. From the start, you must know the risks that you will face in your chosen venture.

If you want to be more creative and innovative in your business, you must take risks to achieve a better result and higher entrepreneurship success.

4. Be a Trooper

A trooper is someone who exhibits extreme perseverance. To achieve entrepreneur success, "Never give up." Putting up a business is easy but managing and handling it is a different story. You must face challenges, problems, risks, and shortcomings but these are normal. The secret is perseverance. Whatever circumstances you meet along the way, never give up.

Everyone has the talent and skills to start his own business but not everyone can be an entrepreneur. You must have these entrepreneur attitudes to reach entrepreneurship success.

Success Secrets from Business Experts

Many business owners are often asked questions about the secrets to their company's success. Many of their replies would include things like having passion for the kind of work that you do or working extra hard at achieving your dreams.

While these pieces of advice are useful and very much true, some people might want to get answers that are a little bit more specific. The truth is that the secret of success is not just one exact event or action from your end but a series of positive actions and a bit of luck. One thing is for sure: it will take a lot of hard work in order for you to succeed. Only a few hundred people were able to succeed in life instantly. Everyone else, even the owners of big companies today, started out small and worked their way into becoming the great business experts that they are today.

It's Really Not a Secret

Many experts in business and successful business owners would often tell you that there really are no secrets of success in business. They would tell you that everything you need to succeed is all in you. It is in your head, in your heart, and in your entire being. This means that you have to have the right mindset and attitude in order to truly succeed in life.

Another thing that successful entrepreneurs would tell you about the secret of their success is that most of their success can be attributed to great ideas, stellar teams, and support from friends and family. If you have all of this, does that mean that you will succeed? The answer is both yes and no. It can be a yes if you do the right things and make the right decisions. It can be a no if you do not do anything about that great idea.

Some successful entrepreneurs would also say that their success is a result of a lot of luck. The truly lucky ones are those who have a good life already handed to them. These are also the people who have the right businesses at the right time. People who succeed in life through luck are those who get a sudden windfall of cash and are able to turn it into something bigger.

So There's No Secret???

Of course there is! But the secret to succeeding in business is not really something that you do not know. In most cases, people already know these not-so-secret tips but do not regularly get to apply them in their daily lives.

Take a look at these tips:

Keep trying even if you fail –

Whether you like it or not, failure and success sometimes go hand in hand. Some people would never experience failure while others would fail repeatedly before they can succeed. The secret here is to keep trying. If you truly believe that your idea has merit, do not give up on it. Tweak your idea until it becomes perfect. Do not accept no for an answer.

Many successful business ideas were rejected several times before they became a success. Some of the most successful people like Jack Ma of Alibaba, for example, applied for admission to Harvard and was rejected 10 times before he was able to get in. He now owns one of the largest retail sites in the world.

Work hard –

This advice is very cliché for most people but it is still true nonetheless. Most successful businesses succeed because their owners worked more than anyone in the company. This often applies to startup companies that have very little manpower to help them get their businesses running.

Working hard means that you are the salesperson, the idea person, the executive, the designer, and sometimes the messenger and delivery person all rolled into one. You have to be ready to take on any kind of task and role in order to succeed. No position is too lowly for anyone who wants to succeed. If you need someone to clean up the mess and do the dirty work, you have to be ready to do it yourself.

Do your research –

90% of the time, good businesses fail because the owners did not do enough research about their product, their market, their competition, and everything that has to do with their business. People who make businesses out of trends and fleeting fads are great examples of people who do not do enough research. They simply go with the bandwagon and hope that their business would take off.

This is not to say that trends cannot become good businesses. People who strike while the iron is hot can still make a ton of money with these businesses. Even if they do not do enough research, the money could still come in simply because these things are in demand. It's a great way to start their business. The research can come later.

Have a good backup system -

While it is true that you can never really plan for everything, having a good backup system will save you tons of money, time, and effort. Make sure that whatever you do, you always have a good fallback, or backup system in case something fails. Diversify your product offerings so that if one does not sell, you still have something else to sell and derive income from. You can also try venturing into a completely different business in order to truly diversify your portfolio. If you are in the restaurant business, for example, try another completely unrelated field like construction or transportation. It might mean that more capital will be needed but it also means that if one of them fails or if you encounter a snag in one of your businesses, the other can easily help keep the other afloat.

Learn from your mistakes – failing hurts.

But it also teaches you a good lesson about your business. Do not be afraid of failure. It will only make you a better businessman if you have experienced what failure feels like. Try to minimize the risk of failure by referring to item #4 and diversifying your businesses. If the idea of failure really terrifies you, you can try getting inspiration from others who have failed and learn from them. Read biographies, personal success stories, and find out how successful people have overcome their trials.

Learn to adapt to changes –

Change is as inevitable as death. You must be willing to go with the changes that your business encounters or risk becoming stagnant and obsolete. Nokia is a good example of this. Nokia used to be the best mobile phone company with billions in revenue for more than a decade. But when smartphone companies started popping up, they stuck with their old phone designs and soon their revenue dropped. Smartphones and other touch screen devices are now reaping the profits that Nokia once had. Being able to adapt to change also means that you have the capacity, the technology, and the know-how. Make sure to keep yourself updated with the latest trends and business practices.

Never stop learning –

One of the most common traits that all successful businessmen have is their unwavering thirst for learning. Even after they have graduated from Ivy League schools and earned their MBAs, successful people never think that they know everything. They would often read and keep up with the latest news and trends. They would try to discover new places and new way of doing things if they feel that this is something that could add value to their businesses. Successful people are always asking questions and wondering about how the world works. They do not shy away from trying new things and trying new technology. They thrive in changes in society and the organization that they work with.

Think positive –

The power of the mind is truly amazing. You can actually will your success or at least make it easier for you to achieve success simply by picturing yourself as successful. This is very hard to believe for some but it is truly possible. How it works may sound like some cuckoo mumbo jumbo but it isn't. The way it works is by picturing in your mind that you have already achieved the success that you crave, your mind will start directing your body to replicate that thought and translate it to reality. Yep, your mind is that powerful.

The power of visualization and positive thinking are your mind's way of easing you into the tough tasks that you will encounter. By visualizing that you have already succeeded, your mind will start to think that every tough thing that you encounter can be conquered.

Make small attainable goals and big amazing goals –

Small attainable goals will help you feel like you are moving forward. Each small achievement gives you something to be proud of. Make small attainable goals in short timelines and work towards your big end goals. This helps you plan out your business strategies and help give you direction.

Create big goals that will help measure your success. Big goals like reaching the 1 Million sales mark or opening a new branch are milestone goals. Make goals big but attainable. Set a good timeline like 3 years for 1 Million sales. Use projections and other forecasting tools to help you determine how much farther you have to work before you achieve your goals.

Reward yourself –

All work and no play makes your life dull. Reward yourself when you reach a significant goal that you aimed for. Go on a vacation every once in a while. Unwind and relax with a good massage or a trip to the beach. Rewarding yourself in this manner helps keep your mind and ideas fresh. It also rejuvenates and energizes you so that you can be ready to take on new challenges.

You do not have to just be an awed admirer of the world's most successful businessmen. You too can be successful in your own craft, field, or expertise. Incorporate these success secrets in your own daily life and be on the same path to success.

18

The Common Mistakes that First Time Entrepreneurs Must Avoid

You will make mistakes. As a person, making mistakes is a normal part of life. The same goes with being an entrepreneur. You are alone in this venture, and you are the lone decision maker as well. Opportunities will present you plenty of events to test your will and determination. Some of these common mistakes are avoidable though.

Picking the Wrong Partner/s

Choose to associate with people who can contribute something different to the group. When it comes to traits, pick people who support what you do. Do not choose friends who will abandon you the moment circumstances get tough. Being stuck with the wrong kinds of people will become the death of your business.

Always Asking for Help

It might occur that you don't have the slightest idea in running a business. In these times, it's okay to ask for guidance from people who had years of experience in running successful enterprises. However, learn to be independent and seek answers on your own. Asking for help a few times wouldn't hurt, but don't commit the mistake of letting other people run your business for you. You still have to call the shots.

Not Asking for Help When You Need It

Of course, you should also know when to bring people in to solve problems beyond your abilities. During these times, it is crucial to let experts have their say so that you don't thrash the business to the ground. The last thing you want to do as a business owner is to be arrogant and to be blind to the problems of your firm. If you let your ego take over, your business might find it hard to recover from its losses.

Hiring the Wrong People

One of the most difficult parts of running a business includes managing people. As an entrepreneur, you have to be vigilant in hiring the right kinds of talents and personality traits to work for you. The wrong kind of people will drive your business down, no matter how great your products or services are. Learn to reward individuals who do their best work. It will increase morale and rapport between you and your employees. Of course, know when to let go of incompetent workers in your business as well.

Obsessing on Your Competition

Allowing yourself to check up on rivals from time to time is okay. But be wary; always thinking of ways to sabotage your competitors may take a toll on your decision-making efforts. Learn to be a fair player. Focus on creating great product offerings, refining services, and adding more value to your business rather than thinking of ways to simply get ahead.

Putting the Customer Last

The most important opinions you must take into consideration belong to your customers. Forget about what your family, friends, or investors say. Make your customers your priority. After all, they are the lifeblood of your business. When researching for the tastes and preferences of your market, go directly to the customers to get data for your business offerings. Never assume unless you have reliable data in your hands.

Running a Bootstrap Operation

Most entrepreneurs are guilty of running bootstrap operations. While the intentions are good, running tight operations might hurt the business venture for it does not allow room for error. Your employees will always have to strive to reach quotas just to make the business float.

It is all about prudence. You know you will make mistakes in your first year. If you have just enough cash to fund each month, you will get in trouble the soonest you fail to reach sales targets. Having enough money in the bank will also help you cushion the fall of low sales expectations.

Getting Too Attached to the Business

It is understandable to feel a close affinity to a business you have built from scratch. However, getting too attached might wreak more havoc than actual advantages for the business. If you get too attached, you will lose your objectivity. Decisions will be clouded with bias and partiality. You can prevent yourself from doing this by asking for feedback regularly. Have someone dependable to tell you the state of your business as is. Lastly, be flexible and gear up for change when the need arises.

19

The 5 Skills Of A Good Entrepreneur

What makes up a good entrepreneur? What are the skills that good entrepreneurs possess? How can these skills be improved? How vital are these skills when it comes to running a business? These are the core questions that we will seek to answer at the end of this book.

We know that being an entrepreneur takes more than just spending money on building a business. It is more than being a boss. Being an entrepreneur is all about creating a culture of values that will lead both the company and the people towards the achievement of personal and corporate goals. An entrepreneur is not only responsible for the business, but he or she is also responsible for the lives of his employees.

A good entrepreneur is not only after profit. Providing lasting customer value is equally important to him. Now what are the 5 skills that make up a good entrepreneur?

- Creativity

- Good working standards

- Creation of product value

- Marketing

- Leadership

It is easy to become an entrepreneur. You just need money that you can invest in your chosen business venture and people to work for you. Once you have these two plus a business permit, you can already call yourself an entrepreneur. However, a good entrepreneur is like a pearl. It takes years of practice and commitment to company policies and goals.

Good entrepreneurs do not only reap a lot of profits but they also earn the trust and loyalty of their employees and customers. Good entrepreneurs create good brands that can last for generations.

The business industry is a wild world and if you are not a good entrepreneur, you will not survive in the wild. Good entrepreneurs know how to deal with people and they take care of people. They know that to be able to stay in the business, they should set priorities and take a lot of risks.

Are you an entrepreneur or a good entrepreneur? Let's find out…

Skill 1

Creativity: Why does it Matter to Good Entrepreneurs?

What is the most essential trait of a good entrepreneur? Many people will definitely claim that leadership is the most important trait of an entrepreneur. Leadership guides the people and the company towards success. Some people will also argue that passion is the most important trait for without passion, success will not be possible. However, others believe that creativity is the most important of them all. Creating possibilities and innovation makes a company stable and creativity makes it possible. A creative mind knows no boundaries and seeing the world in a different light is crucial to company's success.

Why is creativity important to good entrepreneurs?

Creativity is important for so many reasons. These are:

1. Creativity is acquired not born with: People say that artists are born with artistic talents. Yes, it is true. People are born with innate talents. However, creativity is not only about art. It is about making possibilities happen out of nothing. It is about constant innovation through one's imagination. Everyone has the potential to be creative. The mind is so powerful that it can be strengthened and improved.

Creative minds do not break in times of adversity. Instead, they make solutions to problems. Creative people know that there are always 6 ways out of a box. They will not stand there and wait for someone to rescue them. They will try as many possible solutions as they can and only then can they find the best solution to the problem and use it.

2. Creativity is better than intelligence: Most people have this connotation that if a person is intelligent, he has a higher chance of being successful in life. The truth is, intelligence is for the employees to possess and not for good entrepreneurs. What does it mean?

Success is not determined by how intelligent you are as a person. No matter how intelligent you are, if you are not creative, nothing will come out of your mind. Your ideas will remain ideas. However, if you are creative, your ideas will become reality. So intelligence is only for the employees...creativity is for entrepreneurs...because good entrepreneurs make things happen. This, however, does not mean that you don't need intelligence, no. As a matter of fact, creativity is a sign of intelligence so if you are creative, you are also intelligent. Intelligence is not only reflected in the academic achievements but also on how a person solves a problem at hand.

3. Creativity is divergence and convergence combined: A divergent mind has the ability to explore numerous possibilities for problem-solving. A convergent mind, on the other hand, focuses and analyzes the best solution to the problem. To be creative, one needs to look beyond the obvious. There are many ways to solve a problem but a good entrepreneur sees the best solution and he does it.

How to improve creativity:

There are a lot of ways for a person to improve his creativity:

1. Enhance your imagination - Imagination is the first step to innovation. Creating something out of nothing does not happen in just one click. One needs to form an idea and then make it a reality so in order to create something of value, an entrepreneur needs to have a very good imagination.

2. Visualize - All successful entrepreneurs and business tycoons believe that visualization led them to where they are now. Visualizing how your future will be makes it easier for you to focus on your goals and achieve them. Without a vision, a company will not be able to prosper.

3. Experiment on different strategies on how to complete a specific project - One strategy is not always enough to complete a project. There is always a better strategy to use and a good en-

trepreneur knows which strategy works best for a specific project.

4. Train your mind to be constantly active by doing mind -enriching activities like cross-word puzzles, Sudoku, word games etc. If the mind is constantly active, it remains sharp. However, it is also important to rest your mind once in a while; otherwise, you will burn yourself out and you will not be able to perform effectively.

5. Learn to recognize usual patterns in unusual objects put together.

Skill 2

Work Ethics: Getting Things Done

A good entrepreneur should have good working standards, period.

When we say ethics, whether it is medicine, law, business or any other professional disciplines, it is always defined as a set of standards governing the norms of society. Ethics is derived from universal set of values; thus, it starts in the most basic unit of society which is the family. Good entrepreneurs were taught at a very young age the importance of moral values.

In school, they learned to cultivate these values and incorporate them in their lives. These values are: trust and honesty, service and respect for others, loyalty and truth, justice and wisdom, moderation and prudence.

In business, good work ethics becomes a clash of moral values. Ethics in business is not only a philosophical concept. It always requires an action. Entrepreneurs need to do things - the right things. However, there are times, when the right thing to do means bending the law. For example, a business owner chooses to bribe to obtain a business contract just so his workers will still have a job. No business contract means no profit and that means laying-off a number of workers.

It is certainly not right to bribe but is laying-off some workers better? In business, ethics is not merely concerned about what is right and what is wrong. It is more of a consciousness about business obligations, human values and moral standards.

How to Attain Good Work Ethics?

1. Set priorities: For a business to keep on running, the owner must set priorities based in the order of importance and not in the sense of urgency. Learning to identify the most important aspects of the business makes it easier to manage business concerns. Do not give in to urgency but learn to treat important matters urgently.

2. Communicate and align personal and corporate goals: Corporate goals should be communicated properly and must be effectively understood by both the employees and business owners. These goals should also be aligned to one's personal goals to ensure personal growth and success within the company.

3. Ensure balance between work and life: Good working standards call for a balance between one's personal life and career. Some people focus on building and stabilizing their career that they forget what's more important in their life. There are people who fell in love so deeply with their work that they have forgotten what it's like to go out and have fun. Good entrepreneurs have time for their business and they still see to it that they have quality time with their families and loved

ones.

4. Strive for excellence: Every good entrepreneur aims to achieve excellence. It is not enough to perform if it is possible to be on top. Good entrepreneurs strive for excellence because they don't want their company to be just "average". Good work ethics requires an entrepreneur to beat their competition. Customers crave for excellence and if the company is not good enough, customer loyalty will be difficult to establish. Excellence makes successful brands.

Skill 3

Creating Value with Products

Whenever we attend company meetings and conferences, we always hear the word "product value". This, however, does not only refer to the product price per se, but it also entails the quality of the product and how customers perceive its value.

Sales talk is boring to customers if they cannot see the real value of the product. The sales agent should not just talk about the features of their product and services but more importantly, they should also strive to create a connection between the benefits of their products and services to the needs of the customers. Good sales people know how to position the company's products and services in such a way that the customer will see the value of the product, thereby motivating them to buy it.

When a customer sees the product value, price becomes less important. That is why most reliable companies and most stable brands are not really that cheap because their product value surpassed their product price.

How to create product value?

1. Know the customers: When it comes to product value, customers are the most important factors to consider. A good and successful entrepreneur knows his customers. He knows what his customers are looking for and what his customers' needs are. Before an entrepreneur can launch a product or service, he should already know his target market.

He should be able to get inside their customer's head and perceive what they value. By understanding and perceiving the customer value, the business owner can make specific strategies and tactics on how to lure customers to patronize his products and services. People have different needs and wants but a good and successful entrepreneur sees the common interest.

2. Establish rapport: If you want to know what customers really value, knowing them is not enough. One should be able to build a connection and only then a customer will open up. In the sales industry, the sales clerk builds a strong connection with the customer in order to gain a customer's trust. Building rapport is never easy though. Customers are too smart to know that you are just after sales conversion.

To build rapport, it is important to learn how to empathize. This way, you understand what the customer is going through and from there, you can position the "solutions" to your customer problems by incorporating your products and services.

3. Build lasting value: Building a lasting product value is easier said than done, but what really matters is that the customers see the importance of the product and what it can do to improve their life.

Customers look for proof, so you need to be ready to show some proof on how effective your products and services are. You also need to bear in mind that each customer is different, so a different approach is always necessary.

These are the things that you need to remember to build lasting product value:
- Know the situation your customers are in,
- How strong the relationships among your buying team,
- The right questions to ask,
- The customer's lifestyles
- And their ability to tolerate changes.

Skill 4

Mastering the Art of Marketing and Sales

Good entrepreneurs know the importance of marketing. Some business owners are not very excited about promoting their products because they think selling themselves to the customers is embarrassing. Well, if you have a lot of money, you can just hire a marketing company and let them do the work for you. That is why a lot of marketing agencies are hired by big companies whenever they need to do a product launch.

However, if you are just starting to build your own business, you need to do all the marketing jobs yourself and without promotion, your business is just a name and a website without profit...

Here are the three important things you need to consider to ensure that marketing leads to product sales

and customer value:

1. Business objectives: Before marketing your product, ask yourself first "what do you aim to achieve with your products and services?" What is your goal? Do you want to be known for product quality? Do you want your customers to see your company as a company that sells stylish products with good quality and affordable prices? Do you aim to make the business running for a long time or is it just for this season? You need to ask yourself these questions before you can really target a specific audience.

2. Who are your customers: After deciding and enumerating your company's objectives, you need to identify your target market. Who are your target customers? Is it the female population? Is it the students? Do you want to cater to vegetarians? Do you want to focus on real estate development? Are you into sales of ladies apparel? Do you prefer to focus on musical instruments? Are you more of an expert in pharmacy?

You see, there are a lot of possible markets out there. It depends on which market you are going to focus on. Some entrepreneurs believe that targeting multiple markets in just one blow gives the company more chances of generating huge profits. The truth is, the more focused your target market is, the more stable your income gets. You want your company to be known for something.

For example, if you want to be known as the best sushi place in town, then you better focus on making sushi. If you want to be the best vegetarian restaurant, then strive to improve your vegetarian menus on a daily basis. That does not mean you can't innovate. Focusing on one's specialty makes a lot of room for innovations.

3. How can you generate profits? Business should lead to profits all the

time. If you are not making money, then you are not running a business. You are merely doing something like a hobby. In order to master the art of marketing, you need to know ways to generate profits. Marketing can surely bring you sales but without an appropriate platform to launch the product, your target audience will not be able to find you.

It is best to use social media platforms and print advertisements like magazines and broadsheets. Billboards are really effective, and flyers can go a long way. Once you have considered these three factors, your business will surely prosper.

10 Reasons Why You Should Learn Sales

"Don't go to work to work, go to work to prosper," is the advice of Grant Cardone. Cardone graduated college set on a career in accounting but then changed course to work in automobile sales. He didn't believe himself to be a salesperson, but he persevered and made himself one. Now, he has seven best-selling books on sales, is a successful real estate investor and entrepreneur, and is a celebrated motivational speaker and trainer. His story is the perfect example to show that anyone can be a sales expert with commitment and hard work.

Sales is a field that most people are hesitant to venture into, due to the misconception that because they don't have the natural ability to sell, they will never succeed. The truth is, selling is not an innate talent; it is a skill that you can learn and practice. You don't need to have a marketing degree or business background; anyone can be a salesperson with the right mindset – that is, a commitment to hard work, pushing boundaries, and constant learning.

Here are ten reasons why learning how to sell is important not just to make money and get rich, but to grow as a person:

1. You gain confidence.

Salespeople always sound like they know what they're talking about. They make you believe in and trust what they're saying. You may not be naturally confident, but as you continue your selling endeavors, you will slowly become more and more confident with your knowledge about the product or service you're selling, with your understanding of your potential customer or client, and with your ability as a salesperson. Until then, fake it till you make it.

2. You understand people better.

A bit of psychology is always involved in selling, because you are dealing with people. You have to figure out people's wants, needs, and problems – which sometimes they don't even realize yet themselves – and you have to be able to offer solutions, as well as be able to communicate these well. Through selling, you become more perceptive to things such as body language. You become a better listener, and you learn how to ask the right questions.

3. You learn important soft skills.

The sales process can often be a long, tedious one, involving a lot of back and forth between you and the prospective buyer. As you deal with different types of people, you will develop necessary soft skills to succeed in closing a sale. These include communication, presentation, persuasion, negotiation, and decision-making skills.

4. If you can sell something, you can sell anything.

The learnings you gain from working in sales is applicable in any industry. The abovementioned soft skills you learn can be used in to sell any product or service. Therefore, this means that it will not at all be a problem if you, for example, sell pharmaceuticals, and you decide to shift industry and sell houses instead. Once you know how to sell, you can sell absolutely anything under the sun to anyone.

5. You can start out with a sideline job for supplemental income.

If you are not ready yet to devote your entire time to selling, you can always try it out as a sideline job first. The best thing about most sales jobs is that you are in control of your own time, and that the rewards you reap is proportionate to the amount of work you put in. Practice and practice until sales talk feels not only comfortable to you but natural.

6. You can pitch ideas and get support.

Whether in your professional or personal life, you will have to use selling skills to propose ideas to other people, usually people of a higher authority who could support you in getting your proposal approved. This could be a proposal for financial backing to support your passion project or cause, or a proposal for a salary raise, or a proposal to upgrade your mobile data plan.

7. You can build your own business.

If you're thinking of starting your own business, selling abilities are essential. Even from the beginning, you need to be able to sell the concept of your business to potential investors, and then sell your product or service to the target market. No matter how great your concept, it doesn't matter if no one buys what you're offering; a business thrives through sales.

8. You can get rich.

Once you have mastered the art of selling, the likelihood of you earning a lot of money and getting rich is high. Excellent selling skills can open up many opportunities for you: significant commissions, corporate career promotion, lucrative business partnerships and deals, etc. If you look at most wealthy people, the secret to their success and how to get rich is usually taking a great idea and selling it really, really well.

9. You build connections with others.

Selling isn't always about money. Through your interactions with different kinds of people from different walks of life, you will be able to build invaluable and long-lasting connections. You will also have the opportunity to learn and exchange ideas and opinions with others, thus helping you to be a better-rounded person.

10. You need to know how to sell to survive.

Grant Cardone said that he got into sales so that he could survive. It's not all just about making money. You need to know how to sell in your everyday life, so that you can get what you want. When you ask someone for a loan, you need to sell to that person the benefits they will get out of giving you a loan. When you apply for a job, you need to sell to the interviewer your skills and convince him or her that you are the perfect candidate for the job. When you are on a date, you need to sell your personality to your date so that you can get a shot at a second date. You need to sell for survival, and you need to sell well to win at life.

The most essential thing to remember is: sales skills are not something you're born with; they are learned. Learning requires constant studying and practice. While the selling experience is always on a case-to-case basis, you can learn to sell and other important tips and tricks that are generally applicable to most people.

Bottom line is: you really need a strong commitment to learning in order to develop your sales skills and become not only a successful salesperson but a successful business person and entrepreneur.

Skill 5

Being a Leader in your Field of Entrepreneurship

Entrepreneurs are leaders in their own right. However, leadership is not only about titles. Leadership means guiding people towards the common goal and it will not be easy when people do not believe in you. To earn someone's trust takes a lot of effort, sacrifice, motivation, time and convincing power. Unfortunately, it only takes one big mistake to destroy that.

Good leaders have good followers. People listen to the person they trust and they obey their leader. If the people do not respect you, no matter what you do or what you say to them, they will not follow you. As an entrepreneur, you need to realize that the company does not revolve around you. The company revolves around the employees and your customers. Your role is to guide your employees towards the achievement of both personal and business goals.

5 Essential Characteristics of a Good Leader:

1. A leader should be credible:

Credibility is one of the most important traits that leaders have to possess. If you want people to patronize your company and the products and services you provide, you need to maintain a good reputation. Leaders need to be credible to effectively communicate with their subordinates. In order to be credible, a leader should do what he says. Breaking promises and company's rules and regulations will merit distrust and will break people's loyalty not only to him as a leader but to the company in general.

2. A leader should be an expert in his own field:

Being an expert does not mean you need to be all-knowing. Being an expert in the field means being able to see things that are not going well for the company and finding solutions to solve such problems. An expert knows what he is doing. In order for people to follow you, they need to know that you know what you are doing.

3. A leader is a visionary:

Bill Gates, the richest man in the world and the owner of Microsoft - one of the most stable companies in the world started with a vision. He knew from the very beginning that even if the technology is not so advanced in the late 70's, the potential for a computer and software to be a big business in the future is very high. He took the first radical step and now his business has earned him billions and billions of dollars in profit.

4. A leader is not afraid to take the risk:

Every good leader knows that risks are part of the game. They are not afraid to take drastic measures if needed. They are brave enough to try something new and if they fail, they are able to start again. Calculating the risks and preparing for the worst case scenario is one essential characteristic of a good leader and a successful entrepreneur. Warren Buffet and other investors always take the risk but they always manage to succeed.

5. A good leader is a good follower:

You cannot lead where you do not follow. Good leaders lead by examples and for that, they need to be good followers too. If you want your employees to come early, you need to be in your office early as well. If you want your employees to work harder, you need to work hard yourself. If you lead by example, it will not be difficult for you to make people listen. They will just follow you without you telling them to.

20

The Startup Business

Getting out of the rat race and gaining financial stability only has one solution – that is, to start your own business. However, this solution is not a path that everyone can walk on. This is because not all people are able to take the first step and establish their own business – it may be due to lack of funds or lack of knowledge on how to establish a startup business.

This chapter aims to give information about how anyone can properly establish their startup business. Aside from the basics of this concept, it will also discuss the important elements that will make it successful.

What you need to know about a startup business

Establishing your own business is one of the proven ways to bring financial stability to any person. However, not all people know how to set up their startup business as a way to achieve this goal.

This chapter will aim to discuss what this concept is about along with the basics surrounding it.

What is a startup business?

Whether you call it startup business, Startup Company, or startup alone, all of these terms only have one meaning. This concept refers to any business establishment that is still on its initial phase of operation. Startups aim to discover niches or fields in the market that can give profit to its originators.

What makes it different?

Although all businesses go through the initial phase of operation and always engage in researching the market, startups are still different from the usual form of (or non-startup) business.

The following points explain how these two are different:

Startup businesses can be temporary –

Unlike non-startup businesses, a startup could only be temporary. Think of it as a "hit and miss" activity, where the startup's originator presents an idea that may become an important product or service in the market when developed. If it goes well and somebody invests on the idea so that its end result can be reached, then they will gain funds and possible good profit from it should they wish to sell it (more of this on the succeeding chapters); otherwise, they abandon the business idea and will think of another concept for a startup business (after all, only a small amount of money was lost since it's still on the initial phase). On the other hand, non-startup businesses rely on the results of feasibility studies to see if their idea will bring them good sales before it is to be established.

Startup businesses rely on investors and outside financers –

One explanation as to why startups are temporary is that the funds needed for its operation depends on how many people will invest or how much will be invested for the development of the product or service. This is because most startup businesses require a large amount of capital before it can proceed with the succeeding phases of a business (mass production of the product or finding people who are capable of providing the service). Non-startup businesses, on the other hand, rely on the owner's funds (personally or through loans) to proceed with its operations.

Some of the systems that can be seen in an organization are absent in a startup business –

Unlike full-fledged business organizations, some startup types has a loose system. This is due to the fact that the latter only maintains a small team whose focus is on the development of the product or service – this is done so that the business concept can be pitched perfectly and, in turn, gains the attention of potential investors. Thus, there is no need to develop a detailed manual regarding rules and regulations or even develop of a good organizational structure for startup businesses. Only when the startup gains investments and is developed into an actual business organization that they should think of developing these systems.

Benefits of a startup business

Establishing a startup business does have its benefits, as explained on the following points:

There is low risk on your money –

A startup is something that you can engage in if you have the idea or concept but do not have the money to start it alone. Startups rely on presentations to gain investors; since you only maintain a few people to work for you during the development of the business idea or presentation, your limited budget will still suffice even if the concept did not go well.

It can be continued as a large organization –

Once you have enticed an investor to provide the budget that you need for the development of your business idea, you can continue the startup into a large organization. This is especially true if the concept that you have introduced is something that you are also interested with. Since it is your idea in the first place, it is assumed that you know how to make the business more marketable to consumers and be able to solve any problem that you might encounter.

You have the option to sell your idea and gain profit from it -

As mentioned on the previous section, most startup companies are temporary; not only due to its abandonment when it fails, but also when it has successfully attracted an investor. This is because as the one who conceived the idea, you have the right to sell your right/claim over the ownership of the business to the interested investor. By doing so, you get not only a good amount of money as payment for their "takeover" on your business but also the opportunity to work on another startup business or start an actual organization that is aligned to your interests.

Now that you have learned the basics on what a startup business is all about, the next section in this chapter will highlight the steps that you should take if you want the startup to become successful.

Learning what type of startup business are you starting

If you think startup businesses are same, you're wrong. This is because each business idea belongs to one of these business startup types.

This section will discuss what these types are. By knowing them, you get to know more about the appropriate system that you should use in order to increase your startup's chances of being successful.

As mentioned, knowing which type your startup business belongs can improve its chance for success. This is because in each startup type, there is an appropriate system that you should follow if you want it to end successfully. There may also be differences when it comes to key factors in your startup; some of these include the people that you should employ or work with (knowing who is fit for the job), the funds that it needs (what amount or equipment do you need), and other strategies that you need to use. By learning where does your startup belong, you will be able to change your system on these key areas and ensure success.

Your startup can fall in one of these six types:

Business startup for your lifestyle or passion –

Just as the name suggests, this startup type refers to businesses that you've started which is based on things that you have an interest. Typically, these types of businesses are small; after all, the aim of the owner is that they are doing something that they want while earning money from it. The earnings may not be very good, but it fulfills the owner's need. Those who engage in freelance work such as writing or making crafts are examples of startup businesses that fall under this type.

Buyable business startup –

There are also business concepts that are bound to be sold to investors in the future, hence the name "buyable". One guideline that you can use to see if your startup is under this type is if it takes too much time and effort for you to provide the product or service but doesn't give you an equitable profit given what you've spent on it. If you think that the product or service can do better when it comes to sales but you cannot reach the said target due to budget or equipment limitations and the like, you can look for a large company who can buy the startup and make it more successful in exchange for paying you a good amount of money. One example of this business startup is when you are able to develop a Web and mobile application. You may be able to make the app, but its maintenance can be bothersome (fixing bugs, changing interface, etc). This leads the developers to sell it to investors who can do the maintenance and give the right to sell it to their customers.

Small business startup –

This is the most common type of startup. If you want to establish a business with the goal of providing income for you and your family, your business startup is under this type. In this startup type, the funds mostly come from the owner and a few people (mostly family and friends). Another distinguishing feature of this startup type is that the owner doesn't have an interest (and does not make an effort) to sell the business to an investor. Unlike lifestyle startups however, this type earns enough profit. There may also be a need to hire people for this type of business. Small startups, however, do not maintain small for the rest of its existence. Should the owner wish to expand it, he or she can freely do so (although this is not the top priority of those who establish this kind of startup). Some examples of this startup business are grocery stores, consultancy firms, and home improvement companies.

Large business startups –

You also have the option to start a large business right from the beginning. Although it is mostly avoided by aspiring owners due to the very high risk that it carries, the product or service that you will be delivering somehow dictates the type where your startup will belong. For example, car companies cannot be a small business startup; this is because for it to manufacture one car, it requires the work of a large team that will assemble the parts and operates the machines. One advantage that it has over its counterpart though, is that large businesses tend to produce a good amount of profit. It can also easily earn the trust of financial providers such as banks (this is because a business cannot become an organization if it doesn't have enough funds), making it easier for them to take out loans needed for their innovation and expansion.

Scalable startup business –

If you have the vision that your small business concept can be further improved and will become an indispensable product or service in the future, then your business is under this startup type. In a scalable business, the product/service should be constantly improved so that it becomes a good source of income. Once the business starts to gain popularity and has proven itself to be a good source of income, its owners can then sell it to interested parties for a very good price (due to its consistency in providing income). This type of business, however, requires more work compared to the previously mentioned types. This is because you will need to hire and maintain the best people for the job so that the product will be of high quality. It also involves risking funds; this is because once your team finds a scalable business niche, they will need more resources such as money to continue with its development and improvement. Some examples of businesses under this startup type are popular websites such as Google, Facebook, Skype, and Twitter.

Social startup business –

This is the least common of all startup types, primarily because most organizations under this type of business startup are non-profit. The goal of social entrepreneurs is to improve the world – not just make money. Different foundations that provide assistance to different kinds of people who need help such as out of school youth or malnourished children are examples of organizations that belong to this type of business. What makes some people engage in this startup (aside from the joy that helping others can give) is that they don't have to pay taxes due to them being non-profit. They can also earn money from pledges or charity work of people such as celebrities.

Now that you have learned about the types of business startups, you can now qualify which type your business concept belongs into. It is through knowing which startup type it belongs that you will be able to formulate the appropriate strategies that is suitable for each type.

<u>Starting your startup business</u>

If making the decision to start a business is hard, learning the proper way on how to start your startup business can be harder. Thus, you need to thoroughly prepare for several things before you start your startup.

Every business needs money to operate. Thus, for your startup to become successful, it needs to determine how much money is needed to start with the operation as well as where you can get it. The amount of money you need depends on the niche that you would want to penetrate. For the source of money, several sources are available.

Once you have the money that you need, make sure that you stick with your budget. As you are establishing a startup business, there is little assurance that it will return the money that you invested in it or it will even yield any profit at all. Thus, before you start, you need to learn how to control your spending. Stick with providing a budget for the essentials. This will help you prepare for emergency situations that may need financing.

Unless you will be working alone in your business, you also need to hire competent and trustworthy team members/employees and business partner. The people who surround you and will help you in operating or managing your business obviously will have an influence on the outcome of your startup. Make sure that whoever it is that you will hire can provide the quality of work that you expect from them.

Hone your social skills

Startup businesses can become more successful if those who manage it can easily interact with people. This will help them to find investors and other networks, as well as entice customers to try out their product or service. Inside the business, your good social skills will translate to better output from your team if you can socialize with them professionally and informally.

Now that you know what is needed to start your business, we will now discuss what you shouldn't be doing if you want your business to flourish.

Enumerating the don'ts in a startup business

It was mentioned earlier that startups carry lower risks, especially those that did not start as a large company. However, it doesn't mean that you can't make your startup fail in itself or that you can be complacent in running the business. After all, who wants to see their efforts wasted?

We will now look at the common mistakes that startup businessmen should avoid. By doing so, they become closer to their goal of making the startup successful.

-Keeping your "big idea" a secret

The first mistake that can make your startup fail is that if you always guard your "business concept" and refuse to share it with others.

Most startup owners are afraid that their "big idea" is all they have – and if somebody knew of it as well, they might act on it first and "steal" their chance from them. Business experts, however, encourage owners to be open in sharing their "big idea" due to the following reasons:

Business is not about ideas; rather, it's about execution – an idea in itself does not make it a business. As long as nobody is acting to turn the idea into an actual product or service, then it can never be considered as a business. Another point that you have to consider is that even if another person will "steal your big idea", the manner on how it will be implemented will be different. Thus, even if another person knows about your business concept, it doesn't guarantee that the method of implementation will bring it success.

Nobody can help you if the idea is closely guarded – if you don't want to divulge even the basic details in your business concept, even business experts cannot help you. It will be difficult for them to give you specific advises or insights if you are not willing to share the details in your business. It would be like telling your doctor that you're experiencing pain but not telling which area in your body is it coming from.

-Loss of Focus

Although a startup can become successful if its owner will always think of new ideas, there will come a time when you need to become intensely focused. Oftentimes, a startup owner has too many ideas that they tend to become lost as to what should they work on or where should they start. This can become disastrous when it comes to implementation.

It is advised that for an aspiring owner to turn his startup into a successful business, they need to maintain focused. Ideas are good and generate innovation; however, if you don't know the areas that you should focus, you will surely stir confusion to your team and ultimately lead it to failure. Know which systems work and stick on it. Or better yet, you can focus on improving this already useful practice rather than think of another idea that may not be as successful as the first. By doing so, you only get to improve or implement the practices that are giving you good results.

-Connecting on investors, not investees

Another common mistake made by startup business owners is that they are more concerned with getting connected with investors. Although this is exactly what they need to gain the capital for their business, there is an easier way to do it. This is to connect with the people that the investors have granted funds before and became successful. Aside from being an easier method of getting introduced to the investor, it also increases the chances that the investor will actually invest in your startup.

The following points will further explain why you need to start building connections with the investee:

The investees will serve as your way to the investor – before these investees became popular and successful, they also experienced the same problem that you're experiencing now (that is, they are also pursuing for people who can invest on them). Since they know what you are experiencing, they may be compelled to help another aspirant who wants to succeed in their business. As long as the product or service that you will be presenting is repeatable and will provide a steady source of income, the investees will be more than happy to "refer" you to their investors. With this, you are able to connect with both the investee and the investor.

You get to learn more from someone who started with a startup – aside from being connected with the investor, you also get to learn something from the investee. This is especially true if you are able to meet an investee that is in the same or similar niche where you want to establish your business.

-Taking too long to launch the business

Most startup owners think that for the business to become truly successful, everything should be perfect from day 1. Although it is true that success depends on the quality of product or service that you deliver, what's most important in a startup business is that it should be able to penetrate the target market as early as possible. As long as the end product is of good quality, the startup will most likely get the attention of customers. They may even want to be updated as to the improvements that you will implement in your business so that they can be provided with a better product/service. Business experts suggest that once you've penetrated the market, it will be easier for you to plan for improvements, get investors, and expand.

-Trying to please everyone

If you want your startup to become successful, you need to realize early that you can never please everyone – customers and your team/employees alike. This is because if you spend too much time just to turn skeptics into supporters or loyal customers of your company, you will be wasting an important resource that could have been spent on improving your relationship with people who already believe in your business, are willing to invest, and will buy your product even without too much persuasion or marketing. Spend your time with people who will lift your business and help it become successful – not on people that you need to woo first in order to get their approval.

Now that you know the common mistakes that may be hindering your startup's success, it's time to do something to correct these practices. By doing so, your startup will be one step closer to being more successful.

Financing options for startup businesses

All types of business, even the smallest ones, need capital in order to start with its operations. In a startup business, it is common practice that the business owner finds an investor who can provide the budget that they need. The term investor, however, is relative. This is because there are many financing options available to anyone who wants to establish their startup.

5 Common Financing Options

Before the person starts seeking for outside help, they should at least try to generate money on their own using the concept of sweat equity.

In sweat equity, you make use of unpaid services as well as labor so that your startup can build its value. These "unpaid services and labor", of course, refers to using your own skills and time – with the business' eventual success as your salary. This lets you save your precious money on other things.

Working for free, though, has its advantages. Since you do not need to look for someone who will work for you, the control as to everything related to the product or service is on you. One business that started with this financing option is Facebook (Mark Zuckerberg and his friends started the site in a Harvard dormitory).

-Family and friends

The first network of people that any businessman has is their family members and circle of friends. Thus, it is also practical that before they start looking for other investors, they should first seek the help of these people.

Asking your family and friends for money to fund your startup business is mostly positive, as they are people who will most likely support you unconditionally. As long as you are able to present proof that your startup is doing well and that it will produce a good amount of profit, they will rarely say no to your request.

One drawback of this option, however, is you need to properly document your dealings with them and clarify the terms of the loan. Since they are closely related to you and are lending you money, they might assume that they are also owners in your startup business.

-Using your savings

If you strongly believe that your startup can be a good source of profit once it was financed, owners can also opt to risk their own money so that the business will be launched as soon as possible. Not only are you in total control of the business (since the concept and the money is yours), you are also careful when it comes to the expenses, making sure that you are only spending on essentials. As long as you know how to keep records and balance your income and expenses, this option can be utilized.

-Venture capital

Another financing option is to look for venture capital firms. These firms operate by providing a large amount of money to be used as capital for your startup business. However, these firms will only take interest in your business if your presentation shows that its development will ensure a high return rate for the investment. They will also invest if your business has a marketable product or service that can generate continuous profit. This is a good financing option for those who are planning to build a large startup business.

Should your business be funded by a VC firm, you also get guidance from business and management experts so that the investment will be maximized and generate a huge profit. One disadvantage of this method, however, is that the firm will be eyeing for a position in the board of directors. This is to closely monitor where the money is going and influence the decisions of other board members as to which projects are most profitable.

-Acquisitions and mergers

If your startup is a buyable or scalable business (see Chapter 2), being acquired or merged by another company will be the source of your money. This is because an acquisition or merger refers to the process in which a large company will be buying or will team up with a small company whose product or service is similar to theirs and can generate a good source of income in itself. One business that experienced this financial method is Instagram.

By learning about the different financing options that you can use to fund your startup business, you can choose accordingly as to which of the above mentioned methods is best for your startup.

Conclusion

Establishing a startup business is not a walk in the park. It involves knowing the basics such as the do's and don'ts, the type of your startup business, and the different financial options that you can utilize to gain funds for the business.

21

Online Entrepreneurship

Why Now Is a Good Time to Be an Online Entrepreneur

With the rise in the number of internet users, the world-wide web has become a new arena for entrepreneurs and aspiring businessmen. The field of entrepreneurship has taken a whole new level by entering the online world.

Online entrepreneurs have begun to emerge, showing people how to get rich in a different way. To keep up with the times and remain competitive, traditional, long-term businesses also entered the scene to make money online.

Having an online business does not only help you earn more money, but could also help you grow as an entrepreneur. Here, we have laid out a number of reasons why you should become an online entrepreneur now, and how you can get rich by starting an online business.

It is less expensive

Starting an online business is less expensive, because it requires a low start-up cost. You do not need to spend your money to buy a physical lot for your business, or build an office that would require you to spend on materials you will need. You also do not need to spend so much on water and electricity bills that you would normally have to include in your budget when owning a physical business, because everything is done online. You can pay less to get a domain name and hosting for your site.

It is easier to start

Building your own business online is easier because you do not need to go through the hassle of going to the site where your establishment is being constructed, and you do not need to worry about looking for a good location that would provide you with an excellent market. All you have to do is create your own account in online website shops, or create your own site and slowly let your business grow by getting more viewers and having ads posted in your site.

It is less risky

The reality is that not everyone who starts a business would end up successful, which is why most people would not risk spending too much on creating a business that would not ensure profits. Creating an online business is less risky, because in case of a major crash in your business, it is easier to get back on your feet since you are not faced with a ton of financial problems like paying for loans and wasted money on materials.

It is easier to manage

Since most of the work you will be doing is done through the internet and on your laptop, online businesses are easier to manage and track. With all the new features and benefits provided by hosting sites, constructing your online business can be done with ease.

You do not have to worry about traffic

One of the perks of having an online business is that you do not have to go out of your house and go through congested cars in order to get to your office. Being an online entrepreneur allows you to work in the comfort of your own home, wearing your favorite comfortable pajamas while drinking a cup of coffee or tea.

Flexible working schedule

Working online gives you a more flexible working schedule, allowing you to work for a few days in a week. When you need to work or monitor your business, all you have to do is open your laptop and get to your task.

You can work anywhere in the world

Imagine going out on vacation with your family when you realize that you forgot to do some unfinished tasks in your business at home. Having an online business would prevent you from having this problem, since you can access your work even when you are on vacation in case of an emergency.

You can provide more efficient work

An online business would help you produce more efficient results, since you get to work on your desired time in your intended number of hours. Also, most people who build online businesses usually build something out of their passion, and when you are doing what you love, you produce better results.

You control your work

Being a new online entrepreneur would usually mean that you start by personally managing all the parts of your business. You become your own boss, and all the work that you've done is credited to no one else but you – your work is truly your own. You build your business the way you want it to be, and you are free to use your creativity when creating your logo, site, name, and so much more.

You help provide jobs

Once your online business has grown and becomes difficult to manage alone, you begin to hire people to help you track and control your business activities. You do not only earn by doing what you love in the comfort of your own home, but you also help the economy by providing jobs.

You have more time to do other things

Flexible working schedules and being your own boss allows you to have more time for yourself. You now have the chance to spend more time with your kids, take some baking lessons, do yoga, walk your dog, go on vacation, and enjoy other leisure activities.

There is a wide range of opportunities

The online world provides new businesses with a ton of opportunities, in order to cater to the different needs of different types of entrepreneurs and consumers. Social media platforms provide new online entrepreneurs with an opportunity to share their newly started businesses in order to increase their market and strengthen their brand. Aside from this, sites have a way of gathering data, in order to determine what your audience are interested in and what they want to buy.

You can earn unlimited income

Unlike working on regular jobs, getting an online business does not require you to work a number of hours in order to earn a certain amount of money. Your productivity in fewer hours is more important than working long hours and producing less. You can engage in income generating and marketing activities in order to earn even when you are asleep. When your business becomes stronger and more reliable, companies would want to invest in your site by promoting their brands in your website, helping you earn 24/7, 365 days a year.

It makes you more productive on the internet

Running an online business, no matter how small, is extremely helpful, especially for those who spend a lot of time on the world-wide web. Having an online business makes you more productive online, instead of just wasting your time playing games or procrastinating.

You can still keep your day job

The good thing about being an online entrepreneur is that you could juggle day tasks while still earning passively online. You do not need to quit your day job once you've started your online business, but most of the time, when businesses grow, online entrepreneurs go hands-on.

You can lower your household and childcare expenses

Since you now spend more time at home, you can cut down on your childcare expenses and watch your kids instead – send them to school, help them with their homework, and spend more time with them. You can also cut down on household expenses by doing some of the housework yourself.

It is easier to build networks

With the abundance of social media users and web surfers, it is much easier for you to build your network for online businesses compared to physical ones.

There's always room for growth

If you are afraid that you are too late to start your online business, you must remember that the online world is still growing, and a lot of different opportunities are in store for various types of entrepreneurs. There will always be newer ways to increase your earning potential; all you have to do is be updated with the latest trends and features. Online businesses will always have room to grow as entrepreneurs explore their interests and establish better things to sell to their audience.

You can reach out to people

Online entrepreneurs have the ability to reach out to people from around the globe and influence them to support their business, depending on how efficient their marketing strategies are. Having an online business could also be an opportunity for you to share your advocacy to the world, and let people participate in your different activities. You get to strengthen your brand and increase your market while promoting something good.

It helps you become more disciplined

Having flexible working schedules and not having to get out of the house to work sounds great, but it could also breed laziness. This is why online entrepreneurs need to learn to be disciplined, in order to ensure that their businesses would flourish. It encourages you to grow as a person and become more responsible and mature.

With a growing access to audiences from around the world, low costs, and so much more, building an online business would be a great move. It's time for you to take the challenge and present your ideas to the world.

How to Get Rich Online

Tired of the cyclical routine in the corporate set-up? Need extra source of income? Got lots of time to kill at home? Thanks to the innovative platforms available on the internet, earning extra income online had become a widely prevalent practice these days.

With just a handy gadget, an internet connection and extra time, anyone can earn extra cash through numerous ways online. From selling, marketing, writing and even trading, versatile opportunities online are available, that would surely help in footing the bills.

Many people choose a home-based online job mainly due to the flexible time it provides and assistance in financial security. It allows for a work-life balance that most 9-5PM desk jobs do not provide.

Instead of wasting time watching videos, or mindlessly browsing through your Facebook News Feed here are ten easy ways to keep the cash flowing, through online opportunities:

(1)YouTube

According to site ranking group Alexa, You Tube is one of the most visited all across the globe. Hence, a lot of so called professional YouTubers have already found a promising source of living through their own channel in the video streaming site. The trick is simple – create a channel, earn followers, get promising hits and get paid for every single ad viewed by the audience from your videos.

Some of the most popular YouTubers like Pewdiepie, Markiplier and Jacksepticeye cater to the younger audience, mainly discussing online games, RPGs and the likes. What makes them effective is their delivery of video blogging that will keep the audience engaged.

The secret? Create an inviting title, make your thumbnail attention grabbing and spark curiosity from your potential viewers.

(2)Blogging

You probably had already come across artsy photos on Instagram, where each and every single clothing is worn in the photo is tagged. In this digital age, blogging has officially become an accepted way of living. A lot of personalities often tagged as **'social media influencers'**, are earning income through blogging. This can either be for travel lifestyle, fashion, food or even beauty. Bloggers write on what the audience would want to read, and they get paid for it.

When you look at your blog, try asking yourself, Could I be making money from this? Of course you can! You've put the hard work and heart into your words; it is time to reap the rewards. While you may feel that throwing some Ads onto your website may be the answer, I'm are here to open your eyes to a whole new world. Luckily, there are several tricks to get you started whether you are a blogging beginner or an expert on the internet.

I got you covered!

The Goal

In the case that you are just getting your blog started, it is very important to monetize your blog. The key goal for your blog is to get a regular traffic stream. There are several ways to get the visitors and keep them coming back for more. You should keep in mind that each blog is different. What one blog may receive in visitors, may be drastically different from your visitors.

You will want to make sure you find a popular niche. People are coming to your blog for one reason, and one reason only. Your readers have questions! Your job is to make sure your blog has the answers. Once you build trust from your readers, it is time for target practice. For your readers, that is!

As you build your blog, be sure to always keep your audience in mind. If your blog is all about you, you may as well just keep a journal. Your blog should include aspects that will be important to your readers. Your audience will each have a specific need, think of the different ways you can offer answers to all of their problems. This is one reason we suggest sticking with one niche. When you try to offer too much, it will become difficult for people to find the answers they are looking for. With a specific niche, it will make monetizing much easier for you. We believe that there is a method for everyone. Check out just some of your options below!

Top Monetizing Methods

Method # 1: Affiliate Sales

If this seems intimidating, don't let it be! In basic terms, you will be getting paid by a recommended product. All you will need to do is link either an online service or a specific product to your blog. When you are getting more and more visitors, there is a higher chance of a reader clicking on the link to purchase something. When this happens, you will get a portion of the sale. See? It is super simple! If you are looking for a quick and simple affiliate sale, check out Amazon. All you do is place a link to the Amazon product, and you are ready to go!

Method # 2: Sell Yourself

Ok, not really. That is illegal. But, you can sell your incredible skills! You are worth more than you could ever imagine. With your blog, you can show your skills off even further and prove yourself to your audience. When you showcase your graphic design skills, coding skills, or even writing skills, it is a fantastic way to make money. When people see your skills live in action, they would be more likely to turn to you for advice. One way to make some extra cash is to offer your talents through coaching and e-courses. You will be surprised how many people will follow you to learn skills such as application designing, or anything that you have to offer!

Method # 3: Sell Products

While some people use a blog to write, others use their blog to sell! When you do it the right way, selling product can be one of the best ways to monetize your blog! While we have discussed selling other people's products, why not sell your own? Of course, you should realize that this is going to take some extra work, but you get what you work for! When you think about it, you will get to keep all of the profit! There are options out there if you don't feel selling a product is up your ally.

First, you could sell a physical product. Remember that your audience is on your blog searching for answers. When you look at your niche, is there a product in the realm to make their lives easier? Is there something that could benefit your life? Most of the time, the answer is absolutely! We live in an instant reward society; there is always room for improvement.

If a physical product isn't for you, try a digital product! We are in a digital age; the options are endless! To start, we suggest writing an eBook. Not much of a writer? There is a ghostwriter for that! If you are more technologically knowledgeable, try offering an application for your readers. In the end, you just want to be sure that everything you sell if affordable. The more you sell, the more you will make between the blog and the product!

Method # 4: Membership

When you look at your blog, you must ask yourself if you have everything you need to offer? When you offer a membership, you will want to make sure your content is enticing enough. The key is to get them hooked enough, that they will pay for a premium service. If you look at Netflix and Spotify, they do the same thing. They offer a free monthly trial, get you addicted to the media, and then you will pay for the premium membership to make it convenient for you. In your case, you will want to give your readers a taste and make them pay for more.

Another way to do this for a blog is to have what is known as "gated content." With this method, your reader will need a subscription to be able to read everything they want on your blog. With this, you will want to be careful. For small blogs, people would probably just find their answers somewhere else. Instead of a subscription, you can offer detailed guides for a small price. This way, you are offering great advice on your blog, but even better advice for a small fee.

Method # 5: Classic Ads

This is the most common way to make money from your blog. We saved this for last as we wanted to show you that there are other ways to make money. While there is a debate on whether or not advertisements work, they will make you money. The key is having a lot of traffic. If your blog isn't super popular, you should try including other revenue sources. One of the most popular options is to use Google AdSense. As soon as you sign up, you will begin to see adverts showing up on your blog. If you are a beginner, this is a fantastic way to dip your toes into making money. As you become more popular, you can graduate to private advertisements and make even more money!

All About the Benefits

At the end of the day, who wouldn't want to make extra money? You are putting the work into it; you might as well get even more out of your effort. On top of making money, you will be making money doing what you love. (Hopefully) As you work harder, remember that you will want to remain dedicated to your blog. Many people have their hearts in the right place, but blogging isn't always easy. On the days that you feel like there is nothing to write about, remind yourself why you are running a blog in the first place. If you truly love the niche, there is always something to write about and to learn. Remind yourself that your people need you. The harder you work to get an audience, the more money you will make. It is all about dedication. Remind yourself that you can do it!

But how does that work exactly?

Blogging, as one of the most effective ways on how to become rich online, mainly works through ad placements on a blogger's site, sponsored content, paid reviews and partnerships. The higher the audience, the higher would be the pay. This is typically measured through analytics such as pay per click, pay per view and outbound clicks. Hence, the more efficient you are in selling the product to your readers, the more likely you would get paid higher.

(3) Freelance Writing

Love writing, but not fit to publish your own manuscript? Why not try freelance writing? The ultimate weapon on online sites and pages are their content – these must always be fresh, updated and informative. Freelance writers are employed to keep these pages relevant, up-to-date and ahead in SERPs, or search engine results page. Being a freelance writer means having the liberty to work anytime, anywhere and at your preferred pace. All you have to do is to sell the brand in a natural sounding manner, incorporate the keywords and ensure readability of your articles.

(4) Selling products

Of course, the internet has also become a great avenue for selling. E-commerce will always be an efficient and convenient way to earn extra income online because it drops all overhead costs involved in putting up a physical store.

This could also be a good way to ignite your business concept. Have a product in mind like clothing, food or even services? The internet can be a good place to test the waters without having to shell out too much capital funds. Becoming an entrepreneur and being able to track your sale easily are among the perks of being an online seller.

Apart from that, the marketing efforts can be easily done through social media sites which are usually free of charge.

(5) Home based social media manager

Always on Facebook? Well, time to turn that Facebook hours into something productive by being a community manager!

Some companies choose to outsource their online marketing activities which are typically done by agencies. These agencies place a professional fee for representing the brand online. However, some businesses – typically the start-ups, choose to hire an individual to do the basic social media community engagement tasks. Usual tasks of an admin of a certain Facebook, Twitter or Instagram page of a brand include providing real-time responses to each query and re-posting content. The key is to boost the reach of the page, cater to its customers, and keep the site updated.

(6) Selling your own video

Love video filming? Why don't you turn that hobby into a money making activity! Selling videos online have become a very common source of income opportunity in the internet. Similar to stock images, videos can also be bought by companies or brands for their own use. Some popular sites to bid out your videos include VHX, Gumroad, Chill, Tinypass, Pivotshare, Redux and of course, YouTube.

(7) Self-Publishing on Amazon

Have you always wanted to be a writer? Getting noticed by publishing houses can be quite a challenge, especially given the tough competition these days. With that, Amazon is here to the rescue! You may now earn money through self-publishing. This is one of the online opportunities that have sparked hope to a lot of writers. For instance, hit series writer EL James sold over 250 thousand copies of her Fifty Shades novels before she became professionally published.

KDP Amazon, is where you can have your book published. Simply prepare a manuscript, create a KDP account, select the box that you intend to be both Kindle and paperback, choose a cover and finally, upload your manuscript. Within a few days, people may start buying your book on Amazon.

Some people choose self-publishing over traditional publishing not merely because of money, but also due to foreign rights and other packages that you receive if all rights and trademark relating to your work is on your hands.

Amazon is one of the biggest online retailers that you are going to find. If you are an author, publishing on Amazon can end up bringing you a lot of money. But, how are you going to be able to make money on Amazon? In this section, we are going to look at how you can make money off your ebooks on Amazon.

Taking advantage of the Kindle platform that Amazon has to offer is going to be one of the best decisions that you are going to make when it comes to publishing books online because it is fairly simple to follow the layout and get your book out across the world for everyone to read. It does not matter if you are publishing for the first time or for the hundredth time because with Amazon, it does not matter. You are going to be able to establish yourself and gather a good following of people by using Amazon to publish.

Whenever you are publishing on Amazon, you are going to want to take advantage of Kindle Direct Publishing or KDP because this is going to get your book published faster than going the traditional Amazon publishing route. Not only that, but you are going to get a larger percentage of sales by using KDP.

You can also make it to where your book is only available for free on KDP. In doing this, you are going to be promoting your fans to tell their friends about your book. Not every Amazon book buyer has KDP so there are going to be people who buy your book the traditional way which means that they are going to be paying the amount that you are wanting for your book. Of course, this is going to depend on the quality of your work as well too.

The first thing that you are going to want to do is find the proper category for your writing. Every category of writing goes through its phases of being popular or not. You do not have to change every time that your category goes through a down phase. However, it is going to be more beneficial to you if you find a category that is going to not only be profitable but is also not going to have much competition. The less competition that you have to beat out, the easier it is going to be for the customer to come to you and buy your book. With that being said, you need to keep in mind that you should be knowledgeable on the category that you are writing about. Do not just write something because there is less competition and you think you can make money in that category.

Should you still be trying to find what you are wanting to write about, you need to see if you are going to actually sell any books if you were to write in that category. There are some things that are not going to do well if they are sold online because people are not interested in that topic. Or, if they are, there is not a very wide audience. You are going to have to be careful with what you decide to write. For example, if you are writing a fiction book about a brother and sister going to the park, you are going to have a small audience of people who are going to be interested and buy your book, but it is not going to last very long.

The title and cover are what sells the book. If your title is not eye-catching, and your cover does not give some indication of the book, then you are not going to sell books. Think of it in terms of what you would want to see on the cover of a book. Would you buy a book on how to fix a car, but has a unicorn on the cover? Chances are that you won't. In fact, you would probably be thinking what on earth does a unicorn have to do with fixing a car!

Once you have decided what it is that you are going to write, you are going to want to write your book. If you do not want to write your book yourself, then you can always hire someone else to do it for you. There are plenty of ghostwriter companies out there that are going to be willing to write your book for a small fee. When you are writing your book, think about the length. The length is going to determine what it is that you are going to price your book at. Many books are not going to be hard to write and can usually be written inside of a week depending on the topic.

Publishing. As we mentioned before, publishing with Amazon is not hard. In fact, they walk you through the steps on how you will publish your book. It is not going to be published right away because Amazon goes over it before it is published. The most important things you will need to have before your book is published is the book's title, cover, description. And, of course, the book itself. When you are choosing your royalties, you are going to see that you can either get 35% or 70% of the profits. Amazon will determine which one you are going to get based on what you are going to price your book at. You will also need to determine if you want your book to be available throughout the entire world or in certain parts of the world.

One thing that makes or breaks a book is the reviews that it gets. You will have noticed that with Amazon, there are two different types of reviews, the ones that you are going to want to get more of are the verified reviews because these are the ones that mean that your book was bought by an Amazon customer. The more reviews you get and the better the reviews are, the higher you are going to be on the Amazon ranking system. The higher that you are, the more likely it is that your book is going to be found by Amazon customers when they do their searches.

Amazon offers promotions where your book will be offered for a cheaper price or is put at the top of searches for a short period of time. It is going to be up to you as to how you take advantage of Amazon's promotion's that they offer. If you do not want to take advantage of them, you do not have to. You can always do your own promotion and this is going to help push people towards your book as well. Some of the things that Amazon offers are

KDP: this is going to be where you can put your book up for free as well as be able to put your book on the countdown deals. The bad thing about KDP Select is that your book cannot be published anywhere else on the web while it is enrolled in this program.

Countdown deals: your book can go up for a discounted price as we have discussed. So, if your book is $3.00 and you want to give your readers a discount but not a permanent one, you are going to be able to use countdown deals to discount your book for as long as you want it discounted before it goes back to your normal price.

Publishing on Amazon is a great way that you can make money with your ebook.

In the end, write whatever you want to write because you are going to make money off of it as long as your writing quality is good and you market your book properly.

(8) Affiliate Marketing

You have probably come across someone who's been trying to sell something and attempted recruiting you as part of their group? Affiliate marketing, a type of a multi-level marketing scheme, is also prevalent in the online world. The online version is much more convenient than the traditional one. It typically involves enrolling in an affiliate marketing group, selling the product through clicks, links and posts, and earning through a click per share basis. This is somewhat similar to blogging and internet marketing, except that this works under a specific system or group. Think of it this way –for every click translated into a sale, and for every additional recruit to the team, you get a commission straight to your pocket. How does that sound?

Here's How ClickBank Can Help You Earn More

ClickBank's affiliate marketing program is a good way to earn additional income. It's a preferred program by online marketers because it's not complicated to understand. It's an ideal source of passive income because you just need to follow the rules and the commissions will then come.

Before anything else, what is ClickBank?

What Is Clickbank?

Founded in San Diego, California, ClickBank is an affiliate marketing company handling physical and digital products. It's a website that consumers go to if they wish to buy items such as eBooks and various software programs.

What ClickBank does is to act as a middle man between content creators and affiliate marketers. It's in charge of calculating tax charges, checking payments and providing customer service duties.

ClickBank can benefit three groups of people:

The customers, by providing them the items that they need, **the product creators** who come up with the objects that solve the consumers' needs **and the affiliate marketers** also benefit by gaining commissions from the sales of the products to the consumers.

Today, ClickBank is one of the top affiliate networks and is a well-trusted Internet retailer. It assists in generating revenue for affiliate marketers and has reached 200 million customers worldwide.

A Good Marketing Strategy

Choosing ClickBank as an affiliate marketing partner is a good strategy as it can easily manage around 30,000 digital sales each day. It also has 6 million registered users who promote the site's digital programs.

As of 2011, ClickBank has been able to provide assistance to more than 600 countries and has managed to promote around 46,000 products.

How to make money online through ClickBank?

You can create your own product and use ClickBank to sell it, or
You can be a ClickBank affiliate. i.e. someone who sells products in ClickBank's behalf.

If you don't have a product to sell, then opt to be an affiliate instead and still make money. How? Promote the products on your site and lead the interested prospects back to ClickBank. Once the prospect completes the sale, then you get a commission from it.

Many affiliate marketers are satisfied with their venture with Click-Bank. The company makes sure that the marketers are paid promptly and accurately. They are even provided with helpful analytics, enabling them to study their earnings, and get into partnerships to produce higher sales and get better commissions.

Making Money from Clickbank

How to make money online through Clickbank? Just follow these steps to get you started.

1- Choose the product you're going to sell.

It won't be easy to choose a product – after all, the company literally has thousands of them – but to make the task less difficult, pick out one that fits your site or your interests the most. Doing this will also make it easier for you to promote the product.

In choosing the product, there are different factors to consider:

Gravity – This refers to the number of affiliate marketers who are already promoting the product. If there are too many of you who are promoting the item, then it would be better choose a different item to advertise.

Dollar per Sale – How much will you make for each sale?
   Average Percent per Sale – How much commission will the vendor will be giving for every sale?

Take note of all these factors especially if you're an affiliate marketing beginner. All of these will contribute to successful promotions and excellent sales.

2-Promote your chosen product.

Being able to choose the product does not mean you're all done.
   After you've decided which product you'll be selling, you can now click on the 'Promote' button. After clicking the button, a URL link will pop up. Copy and save the link – this link is what you'll be using to promote the product.
   How will you promote the product? You can use the following tools:

- Your personal blog
- Free classified websites
- Social media sites e.g. Twitter and Facebook
- An article to promote the product
- YouTube videos

- Email and/or search engine marketing

Pick among those methods, find which ones work best for you and use that to endorse your preferred product.

3-Sell and earn from your product.

Now that you've picked out your product and your selling method, it's time to sell and make money using those tools.

Paste the link that you've copied earlier on your site or blog. Once your blog is published, anyone who visits your site and clicks your link will be routed to the product page where they can purchase it.

If the customer ends up buying your product, you'll receive your commission. This amount will be automatically credited to your account. The more products you sell, the more commissions you'll be receiving.

ClickBank will pay you each month once you've reached $100 in your account.

Making the Most of Clickbank

Want to boost your earnings? Try out these tips to help maximize the profits you'll be getting from ClickBank.

Choose a good product that fits your audience. No matter how good your product is, if the right people don't find out about it, then your efforts will be pointless.

Utilize tools to maximize your sales. There are software programs you can use to further improve your sales rates. There are also free tools that you can use if you want no additional charges – the tools allow you to see products with highest gravity rates, popularity, recurring income and other factors.

While it's true that the higher the gravity, the more people are earning, you should also remember that some newly released products have low gravity but are also potential hot sellers. Observe and study the product first to see how it will perform.

Aside from Facebook and Twitter, try out other sites to promote the product such as Pinterest and Instagram. A lot of people are using them, which can lead to more traffic for your site.

Those are just few of the tips you can try out to boost your earnings from ClickBank affiliate marketing. Soon, you'll discover other ways of adding more to your earnings.

Conclusion

Don't be afraid to try out ClickBank. A lot of people have proven its legitimacy in earning commissions from selling products. It's a good source of passive income because all you need is to set up your site, choose products, paste the link, and that's it.

All you need is to find out ways on how to boost your earnings. Once you do, it'll be a good source of proceeds to complement your income.
Don't have an account yet? Visit their site and create your own ClickBank account. Creating an account is free of charge. Soon, you'll earn and receive the commissions from the products that you sell.

(9) Stock Market (Forex)

Apart from the open market which mostly involves equity, forex trading is also a platform where you can earn a lot of money. Foreign exchange, widely known as 'Forex' or 'FX', is the market driven exchange from one specified currency for another at an agreed price being bit through over-the-counter markets worldwide. You can earn money by buying your forex money at a low price, and correspondingly selling it once the market prices turn out higher. Forex is one of the most active markets with an average turnover of about US $5 trillion daily.

How to Make Money as a Forex Trader Online

In the rubble of today's financial crisis's, it is no secret that majority of us have spent countless hours pondering over how we can build a more stable financial foundation for ourselves now, as well as for our inevitable futures. There are many individuals who have spent endless time that we cannot get back glued to the Google search results, hoping for a miraculous answer on ways to make money in honest ways. Perhaps we are all spending too much time searching in the wrong places, and need to view ourselves in a more professional light when it comes how we make and spend our hard earned cash.

You either came across this article during one of your sleepless late-night desperate Google searches, or you are here because you have actually heard and want to hone your skills as an online trader. I know what you are thinking, "Trader?! Nope. Nu-uh. I am not smart enough, nor am I equipped with the green to be able to do such a thing." Well, I am here to tell you to rethink what you "know" about trading.

Yes, the world of trading, let alone virtual trading, can be so broad that it is nauseating. But, have you ever heard of Forex Trading? Well, in a nutshell, this is the umbrella where ALL global currencies trade. That makes for quite the umbrella, but bear with me! With its size comes the title of being the most liquid markets in the world. Forex trading is pretty similar to stock trading, but with one awesome exception. You can conduct Forex trades 24/7! This helps those that do this gain major exposure to international markets.

When it comes to anything in life that is among any complexity, it is vital to have a good understanding and vocabulary on the subject at hand. So, let's dumb Forex trading down and bit, and break it down for better understanding.

Forex is most abbreviated in the terms of "foreign exchange." Both investors and speculators trade within this market. For example, let's compare the good ol' U.S. dollar to a euro. Perhaps the U.S. dollar is foreseen to decline? More than likely in this type of situation a forex trader will sell dollars to purchase euros, for when the euro strengthens, the purchasing power to then buy dollars has increased. Which in turn means the trader can buy back MORE dollars than what they originally had to start out with, making a profit.

The secret to Forex Trading is initially all within the exchange. Exchange rates that is! The foreign exchange market itself is a marketplace that determines the values of different currencies. The existence of currency is more vital in conducting foreign business than any one person realizes. The livelihood behind forex marketing is the need to network! The size of Forex marketing makes other areas of commerce looks sizably smaller, with a traded value of $2,000 billion per DAY. And yes, that is in U.S. dollars. With all that green flying around to different places, you may be wondering how YOU can get in on just a tiny piece of this action! Well, you are in the right place.

If you are to be truly successful in the ways of Forex trading, you are going to need to have a few key know-how's and a couple tricks under your belt to really know what you are doing, especially when your own earnings are at stake. Next are some things to keep in mind from experts in Forex trading themselves!

Analyze Your Needs, Plan Goals and Stick to It!

To be able to receive any profit in the world of trading, you first must know the signs of recognizing markets. But, hold those horses! Before that step, you firstly have to get to know your true self. Understanding your needs can help you define your risk tolerance! Taking the time to ensure that your capital quotas and risk tolerance are in balance and not either excessive or lacking is an important step many people think through too quickly. Studying and analyzing your financial goals and dreams is just as engaging as taking a leap into the actual trading process.

Once you figure out what you initially WANT from trading, you can honestly define your goals and the timeframe you would like to meet those goals. Knowing how much time you can devote to trading is a big step into achieving the goals you want out of this venture. Having concise goals makes it easier to stick to trading, as well as ease in jumping ship if risks overshadow your profit too much for comfort.

Pick Account Type that Works for You

It is important that you choose an account package that as the ability to leverage ratios in accordance with your wants, needs and expectations of trading. This step can be a bit confusing, especially as a beginner. The general rule to follow is the lower the leverage, the better the bet. For beginners it is recommended that a period of studying and practicing how a certain account may leverage happens before really committing to an account type. This can be done by the utilization of a mini account. The rule of thumb: the lower the risk, the higher your chances. So it is smart to be conservative as a beginner in this field.

Bigger is Not Always Best

An ounce of wisdom in getting your feet wet with Forex trading is learning that small sums can get you farther than depositing large sums. Small sums equal lower leverages. This does not mean if you are feeling like living on the edge a bit not to do so, but as a beginner it can be wise to start small and see where it gets you. You may be surprised that your tinier investments may get your more profit than those that pump large sums of money into their accounts.

Act On Understanding

Forex trading is not the time to be acting upon things just because you believe you get the "gist" of them. The world of currency is deeply vast and wildly complicated. This is because of the very chaotic nature that markets tend to have. Even for those that are experienced, it is hard to master all the different kinds of financial activity that goes on in the corners of the planet. It is wise to start with the trading of currency you know well, such as your own country. Either that or stick to those trades that are most liquid.

"Success Is Never Permanent and Failure Is Never Fatal"

This quote should be lived by within all aspects of life, but especially in the world of Forex trading. It is important to know that you will fail, probably A LOT, before you really start to get the hang of how it works, and how it can initially work for you! Make sure you take physical or mental notes, studying both your successes and failures. You will start to grasp a deeper understanding from the very first dollar you invest into the circulations of the Forex. Keeping track of all your trading activities, along with hard work, will land you in a sweet spot, all thanks to the ways of Forex marketing!

22

Social Media Marketing For Online Businesses

Before the World Wide Web, businesses depended primarily on "word of mouth" marketing of their business by consumers. This as well as television and radio ads that most consumers tuned out as soon as they began airing, were the primary venues associated with marketing. Today social media outlets have allowed online businesses to get the word out more quickly and efficiently, and have also created a gateway for controlling the image businesses are presenting to the public.

It takes time and patience to build a strong presence for your online business but the perks of social media marketing can be invaluable. Business recognition and quality control are things that could break a marketing budget with traditional marketing techniques. Social media marketing gives you, the business owner, the control and power to drive your success in a more cost-effective manner while also allowing you to create and meet your time constraints.

Business Recognition

Everyone is using social media these days; it's not limited only to connecting with your family and friends. It's everywhere and it's an open avenue for marketing your online business. Social media venues such as Facebook, LinkedIn, Twitter, and Pinterest offer users the ability to specify keywords to target their marketing efforts. Automatically, your ads are being viewed by consumers already interested in what you have to offer. You have now saved money and countless hours of footwork in locating your target audience. While there are some fees involved in promoting or marketing your business through social media, the financial burden is much less than hard copy or printed ads might cost. The business can also control the time of marketing releases to fit their schedule and agenda as opposed to the time constraints associated with print copy.

One major trend is coordinating your business press or marketing releases with what is happening in the world at that particular moment. Because traditional marketing scenarios take time in planning and generating, the moment may be lost in timing. However, the instant publication platform that social media marketing allows, gives you the opportunity to market your business in a timely manner before the moment is lost to an updated news trend. Your online business will soon be perceived as a business that keeps up with the ever changing demands of our world today.

Because you're most likely using these social media outlets for personal reasons, why not begin incorporating the name of your business with your personal information. Most people would prefer to utilize a business they are familiar with on a personal level. This technique offers a feeling of trust and predictability that traditional marketing efforts lack.

When conversations form online and several users who know one another begin to use your name, there is another level of trust that is added to the already familiar business name. This could take months, sometimes years with dated marketing endeavors and your business has managed to produce the same results in a mere fraction of the time it may have taken traditionally.

An important tactic to remember when using social media as your key marketing tool is to become engaged in conversations that involve subjects that target the same issues and ideas that surround your business. Make sure you are participating in conversations by "liking" the points of others within the conversation or contributing positive aspects to the conversation as a mere participant. People have an innate need to be heard and acknowledged. It is extremely important to engage in these online conversations as an interested party and not someone who is simply lurking only to get their business name out there and recognized. Once you have established yourself as a valued participant in conversations, any use of your business name from that point on will be viewed in a more positive light than if you were to use it constantly without invitation or need.

Quality Control

Once your business is recognized on social media outlets you'll want to keep your name associated with positive perceptions by your audience. Even the most successful online businesses have received their fair share of bad publicity or negative comments. Traditional consumers can be leery of online businesses as opposed to store-fronts due to the inability to deal with someone face-to-face. It's important to look at this as an opportunity as opposed to a setback.

Social media has given you a means to address the issue with not only the individual with the complaint but the onlookers who want to know how you resolve dissatisfaction by your consumers. Once again people need to feel acknowledged and validated. That is half the battle in a nutshell. Not only does this simple task defuse a difficult situation, it allows others to see that your business is personal and accountable. We all know that no one is perfect and consumers need businesses to realize that as well.

Once acknowledgment and validation have been offered, you can move on to resolution. This discussion can take place publicly, online, and is invaluable to the business. Consider how many people heard negative things about a business via "word of mouth" but were rarely, if ever, able to witness the resolution. There are cases, however, where the resolution would be better offered privately between the consumer and the business. This can also work to the advantage of the business as it gives the appearance of valuing the disgruntled consumer enough to give them private, personalized attention. Once the consumer is satisfied they're more apt to offer a positive review of your business to those asking about the outcome of the situation during online conversations that will inevitably be taking place.

The Future Of Social Media Marketing

Consumers are now doing everything online from conversing with friends and family to watching movies and keeping up with the news. You can make sure that your business is visible in every online space available for marketing. Social media marketing is a simple tool that will quickly associate your business name with the very people who share an interest in what your business has to offer. Social media marketing is a necessity in today's business world and you can make it work to your advantage by developing your marketing plan utilizing the tools available through social media platforms. The platforms mentioned at the beginning are just a few that are used daily by millions of people. Start by searching social media sites and make a list of what they offer in terms of marketing. You can then coordinate what is available through social media sites with your marketing agenda and business goals.

You now have the power and control you need to successfully market your business utilizing social media as your platform. New online businesses are continuously being established, and even traditional store-front businesses are incorporating the online business model. It has never been more important for your online business to utilize social media marketing than it is today. The decreased financial burden of social media marketing and the increased viewership of social media marketing strategies are growing quickly and the sooner you incorporate these into your business model the faster your business name will be recognized as a pioneer in social media marketing.

Facebook Marketing for Online Business

With billions of users spanning across all possible demographics, it's a no-brainer for any business enterprise, big or small, to carve a presence on Facebook, the world's biggest social media network. The importance of marketing Facebook leaving a footprint on it has become very critical, so much so that an enterprise that isn't on the site probably does not exist at all.

Consider the ordinary Internet user. A person interested in, say, your business would more likely go to Google to look up information about your business. If yours is linked to Facebook, one of the first things that will show up on the search engine results would be the said Facebook page, followed by the official website of your business. Between the two, the ordinary Internet user is likely to click the one relating to Facebook because, let's face it, Facebook is more familiar. Besides, who has time to navigate through a business website?

It goes without saying, therefore, that insofar as marketing initiatives are concerned, having an organization's presence felt by using Facebook for marketing counts as one of the essential must-do's.

There are plenty of reasons why any marketer worth his salt, or any business enterprise for that matter, should not forego Facebook. Here are some of them:

1. Facebook has over a billion users. Yes, billion.

As the largest and arguably the most influential social media site today, it goes without a surprise that Facebook, a site originally designed for college students, now has over a billion users. These users come from all corners of the world: across geographical boundaries, race, age, gender, social strata, and all possible sorts of inclinations. Facebook's demographics are expansive and cover all possible markets.

This fact alone should be enough reason for any business to do marketing through Facebook. However, the number of people on Facebook should not deceive you into believing that by merely being on the site, success automatically follows. It takes more than that.

If anything, Facebook's popularity is indicative of your potential to find your target market, create a fruitful engagement with them, and harness the social media network's functions to eventually translate these connections into profits.

2. Unless you choose to pay for ads, using Facebook is free.

Traditional marketing strategies that utilize print, TV, and radio cost money. Not with Facebook. Signing up for Facebook only requires a valid email and a phone number for security and you should be all set.

Using Facebook for marketing significantly reduces costs, particularly for businesses with very minimal budget allotted for marketing. As such, it works for small enterprises keen on letting the word out on their business but with little money to spare for advertising. For big businesses, creating a Facebook account serves to strengthen their market hold and support further growth.

3. Facebook provides an array of marketing alternatives.

For the uninitiated, a Facebook page is essentially the business equivalent of a person's status feed. A Facebook page is ordinarily what people look at to get an overview of what your business has been up to. It is free to set up, and only requires imagination and creativity to get it rolling.

But quite apart from pages, Facebook likewise provides two other marketing options: groups and ads on Facebook. A Facebook group can either be public or private. It is different from a page in the sense that a group tends to foster discussions or interactions among its members while a page is generally intended to serve as a repository of updates, promos, and other marketing gimmicks. But similar to pages, groups are also free to set up.

Unlike pages and groups, ads on Facebook are not free; businesses that choose to post ads have to pay, depending on the number of clicks or interactions created by the ad.

Of course, the beauty about marketing Facebook is that the ad is directed to your actual target market. With the vast data Facebook has, advertising on the site means you get to decide which people of a certain age living in a certain place will see your ad. The approach is more direct, hence more effective. Ads on Facebook are also less visually obtrusive; ads are displayed in a manner that does not make them annoying. They are also relevant because they are tailor-fitted according to the profile and stated interests of a certain user.

4. Facebook can rack up traffic to your own site.

Once you have created an audience on Facebook, it now becomes much easier to link up your own website. Many businesses post links on their Facebook pages, groups, or ads enticing their audience to click a link which directs to their own website. It's a nifty way to guarantee an increase in traffic on your own site without coming across as hard sell.

5. Marketing through Facebook promotes a strong feedback mechanism.

The good (or bad) thing about Facebook is that anyone's voice can be heard by merely posting a comment. This is good if you want to have an idea of how your market reacts to your business or an aspect of it. Depending on the kind of feedback, you can either continue doing what your customers love, or devise ways to address concerns raised.

Many times, the comments generated by your Facebook account serve as a springboard for others to post their own comments, too. Positive feedback are almost always seconded by others who have had the same wonderful experience. However, it is the negative comments that mostly stir other people's curiosity. Handling these negative comments in a professional manner is key in turning them into opportunities to shine through.

6. Having an account on Facebook is a great way to earn more leads.

By building a page or running ads on Facebook, you get to expand your potential customers or clients. This becomes even more obvious when you engage in marketing strategies, such as contests and signups, where you get to have the email addresses and phone numbers of these people which they have given voluntarily. These information are crucial for marketing and generating sales outside of Facebook. In this sense, Facebook is useful in enabling you to create leads of who may be interested in your business without bombarding their personal Facebook accounts.

7. And finally, marketing Facebook provides a statistical overview of the performance of your business.

Most of all, Facebook provides an Insights page that allows you as a page owner or advertiser to have a statistical overview of how your page or ad is doing. Facebook's Insights works in the same way as Google's Analytics: Both provide data relating to the number of impressions, clicks, views, likes, and the performance of the pages or ads on Facebook that can be managed to display either a daily, weekly, monthly, or even an annual assessment.

While these figures may seem intimidating at first, knowing what they mean is crucial in understanding how your audience reacts and in determining what strategies work and what don't. They are also important because they serve as a sound basis for whatever changes you seek to implement or initiatives you wish to jumpstart.

Given the foregoing, there is little doubt that Facebook is a great starting point to establish your online business. Needless to say, now is as good a time as any to start using Facebook for marketing.

The Power of Facebook Ads

Nowadays, you will hardly meet anyone not on Facebook. The internet is basically an extended arm of a human that is primarily used to interact with other humans in the cyber world. If you are not on Facebook, there is a high chance that you're missing out on the latest trends, the most controversial political news, and the most scandalous celebrity drama that your friends and family are currently tuned into.

However, you would know by now that Facebook is a very powerful tool and it has more uses than just "poking" a friend and hitting "like" on photos you find on your feed. Small enterprises to large corporations use Facebook as a business tool to promote their company's best interest. With Facebook, different kinds of businesses from different kinds of industries are able to build their brands and reach their target markets; even the most unlikely business, such as a law firm, can invest in Facebook to promote their services.

To be precise, law firms can make use of Facebook Ads to give more attention to their profession. What's good about this is there is an almost-untapped market on Facebook since their competitors are still stuck in the past by putting up physical ads on newspapers and yellow pages or even advertising themselves on TV or radio, which tend to be quite pricey. Little do these firms know, but this form of "traditional" mass advertising does not work well anymore and would actually only reach a small portion of people especially since the global shift on how advertisements is presented –this is where social media, a.k.a. The Internet, comes in the picture.

What's a Facebook ad, anyway? How does it work? According to Facebook, the popular social media network has about two billion active users around the world. That makes it a very attractive advertising platform for users to promote and grow their business. Facebook makes it easy to do so with a few simple steps since the social media page provides user-friendly instructions and illustrations for anyone who wish to make use of Facebook ads.

First, they must choose an objective. For a law firm, that would be to attract new clients by building brand awareness and promoting the specific practice areas that they cater to. Choosing the target audience would be next. Given that facebook has a lot of users, the business must determine the people they want to reach. Facebook allows them to customize the audience by demographics, location, interests, and behavior so they know who to show the ads to. Not only do they show this to your desired audience but also to people similar to them which then increases the chances of reaching other users who may be interested in the business. For a firm, it would be wise to target depending on the specific practice area they handle. A firm that specializes in Corporate Law, for example, targets both the consumers and the working class.

Like any other businesses in the world, a law firm should clearly specify in their ad how they are unique from the rest of their competitors. The ad should answer the question, "Why should we hire you in the first place?" But of course, all law firms would claim that they are the best amongst the rest of the law pool; an ad should be able to catch the attention of their audience at first glance. It has been debated that it would only take about four to six seconds for an ad to catch the attention of a human before they move on to the next bright virtual object that distracts them. Since people have very short attention spans, Facebook adheres to the rule to have ads limit their content to 20% text only; meaning, the rest of the ad should be expressed in a different way –through the use of colors and imagery. This rule actually works wonders for viewers who are always on the go. Even if the audience is willing to take an extra few minutes to do research on law firms on Facebook, the one with the most eye-catching ad that is straight to the point would always be the advantageous one. Having Facebook ads is a powerful tool for growing law firms with aims to expand their horizons, since you'll never know who would be needing legal help. Facebook is a place where all kinds of people from all over the world come together. With this tool, law firms who wish to broaden their scope are able to reach international online traffic with only a click of a button.

For businesses like law firms, using Facebook ads is a cost effective way of advertising for many reasons. The firm can set their budget easily and get their money's worth. Law firms usually rely on mass advertising but they don't really know who sees them or who attracts them. Since Facebook allows users to customize their target audience and to focus on them, the advertisement will not be shown to users who have no interest in their service. More importantly, the firm can gather data to see how well their ad is doing. Facebook provides insights and other tools through the adverts manager to help the business understand their market better and create more effective advertisements.

How to Use Instagram to Market your Online Business

Facebook and Twitter are two of the most popular platforms to advertise your product, but marketing on Instagram is starting to gain ground in the industry. You can boost your online business with your Instagram account. What's with Instagram that makes it a great tool for your business?

One, it is popular. As mentioned, it is one of the most widely-used social media platforms today. Aside from its user-friendly interface, it is fairly easy to create advertisements, memes, and virtual flyers and posters with Instagram.

Marketing on Instagram may be your ticket to fame and success, as many Instagram users are shoppers. The virtual community itself is filled with customers who are eager to see something new in the platform and to share whatever is worth their time and money.

Second, Instagram makes brands accessible, as Facebook and Twitter do. Social media marketing has taken online selling and advertising to new heights. In a study in 2015, it was found out that 70 percent of Instagram users look for a brand in the same platform. Perhaps, this is because these users are visual shoppers and they like seeing new products and promos from the brands they are following.

Images are the strongest motivators to shoppers and looking up the IG accounts and posts of brands is tantamount to online shopping. It can be noted that Instagram helps consumers make smarter decisions, and helps entrepreneurs become better sellers.

Why Instagram?

Instagram is not only popular, but it's also useful and easy to manage. Anyone with a smartphone can download the app from Google Playstore, and the fun starts in minutes. Unlike Facebook, IG is not too strict about photos used in advertisements. Consumers can also scroll through your page and browse more products using their Android phones.
    But how do you use social media marketing to boost your business?

The basics: Set up you IG account. This account is for your business and should be separate from your personal interests. Your IG account will target your clients, hence the posts should make them want to see more of your products. Whatever is relevant and meaningful to your customers is what you should focus on. If this means you not appearing on ANY Instagram post, so be it.

Moreover, make sure that the IG account and username match your company's name. The logo of your brand should be the profile picture in your IG account. Because you want to keep the influx of consumers going to your page, being consistent with the profile picture and name will help solidify the consumers' image of your brand. The account name should also be unique.

Second, include a link to attract consumer traffic to your account. The use of hashtags, those phrases and words that are preceded by a number sign (#) can do the trick. When consumers type a certain keyword on the search box, they will be directed to hashtags or links that display the same words. The link may also be your company website. This should be displayed on top of your IG page.

Third, be consistent with the photos. Instagram has the photo filter feature that lets you edit your images. You can play with colors (i.e. make the tone yellowish or sepia) so that the best part of the image is highlighted. A beautifully-written caption should accompany your image. A rule of thumb for businesses is to use the image of a product, a testimonial or a photo of a satisfied customer, and inspirational words that make people think of your products.

Suppose you own a bakeshop, and you want to take photos of your products. You can take advantage of your creativity here. You may emphasize the "Pastry of the Day", showing only one pastry. You may also show a color-coded pastry, for example a treat on Valentine's Day (a slice of red velvet cake, a heart-shaped placemat, and a red mug). You may also use your wit and post a meme that says "How's your bread and butter today?" that can be taken figuratively, but can also be shown as a literal slice of bread with a roll of butter on top. There are so many creative options with Instagram. You only have to think and try what could work for your brand.

Next, write an interesting bio for yourself and an equally interesting description for your brand. This seals the deal with your customers. It's telling them whom they should trust (you) and why they should check out the rest of your photos. Though you can exercise your creative license, you must keep your bio and description light, concise, and to-the-point. You can write about who you are, what you do for a living, and something that would entice readers to buy from you, or at least click the link that you have included.

You may feel proud when people follow your account. It's basically like fangirling. It won't hurt to follow potential customers. Like their photos, especially those that are of the same nature and topic as your business. This is where hashtags come in.

However, Instagram is not the place to do hard-selling. Photos are used creatively to convey images. Sometimes, a text in the image is not necessary, but the careful arrangement of products and other props for your "photo shoot" give your image the " X" factor.

That said, the photos must be of excellent quality – a photo with a high resolution is preferred. It should also be sized properly. The images should also be professional-looking. If possible, images may be edited previously, using more sophisticated and advanced software such as Adobe PowerPoint. Good thing there are apps such as Instasize that can edit the photos quickly.

You may also jumpstart on introducing various promos and announcements in your IG account. Whereas Facebook can upload brochures, flyers, and post longer texts, you have to exercise brevity in Instagram. Again, the image should already speak for the brand, and should promote a positive brand image and culture.

It is likewise important to update your Instagram account often, if not daily. People will always keep an eye on their favorite brands, and they would want to be the first to know if the company has released a new product or promo. Use this 'proactive' attitude in social media shopping to your advantage. You can balance out all the fun and professionalism in your posts. Tell a story with a single picture. Use drama to appeal to the consumers' emotions and logic.

What's good about IG is that it can be connected to Facebook and Twitter. Thus, you can target three social media accounts with just one post. This online marketing strategy is definitely cost-effective and time-saving. You may also post videos on IG now. Shoppers would like to watch demonstrations and testimonials on videos.

If you can, follow back your followers and comment on their photos. If they took photos of your products and linked you to it, return the favor by saying thank you or providing a feedback of appreciation.

The Future of Your Business with Instagram

With more millennials and digital natives forming a huge percentage of consumers, you can only assume that your business may flourish with IG. You have the power to convince your customers to check out your stuff and eventually buy them. IG is a great social media platform to use for your online business. Because everything is so advanced now, it is only a matter of time before Instagram introduces other cool features aside from image resize and photo filters. Instagram is here to stay.

23

Lifestyle Design

The Concept of Lifestyle Design

The Purpose of Living

Do you want to know what lifestyle design is? To do that start by imagining yourself living the life you have always wanted. Doing the things you have always dreamed of when you were a kid? Then, focus on your life right now and start asking serious questions, such as:

1. Are you living the kind of life you dreamed of when you were little?

2. What happened along the way?

3. What makes you happy?

4. What do you love doing?

5. Why are you not living your ideal life yet?

6. What is stopping you from making that leap of faith?

It's likely though, that you are looking for answers and you feel stuck. Count yourself among those who are not getting any fulfillment with the work they are doing. Somewhere along the way, reality hit you hard in the face. As some say, idealists have no place in this world.

You had to find a job. You had to get married early. You had to work to finance the expenses associated with starting a family. You need to buy the biggest house you can afford and, maybe, a car or two. You take vacations at luxurious destinations at least twice a year. This is the "Great American Dream." However, it's not unlikely that you aspired for something a bit different. What if your idea of happiness lies in doing what you love all the days of your life, and that excludes having a boring desk job? Welcome to the newest concept in town that might have the answers you are looking for: lifestyle design.

The Key Idea of Design

The concept has been around for ages. For many years, people have talked about living a lifestyle that is different from what society expects of its citizens. The concept had just been properly labelled when Timothy Feriss published a book entitled, "The 4-Hour Work Week: Escape 9-5, Live Anywhere, and Join the New Rich" in 2007.

The idea behind lifestyle design is to live the unconventional life. Instead of spending your day at your cubicle doing menial or unfulfilling work, you do meaningful tasks – preferably, at an exotic location. Think of it this way: you travel and experience new things while you are earning enough money, doing jobs that create an impact on the greater majority.

That is as idealistic as it can get, but it is slowly becoming the trend nowadays. This means people are getting tired of living a routine each day and conforming to societal expectations. They are looking for new ways to live their life and to the find meaning of their own destinies.

Is the Concept for You?

The answer's both "yes" and "no". The concept's suitability depends on how you think about certain things in life. If you have no trouble accepting the status quo and its expectations, then maybe you are living the life you actually wanted in the first place. You crave security and stability.

If you desire for something greater than the routine of a life you are living, then lifestyle design is for you. Actually, the idea is not really exotic in itself. It basically means to put your life into your own hands and start calling the shots yourself.

It is all about finding what will make you happy. If that's about staying in the office and being part of a corporate organization, then let it be. If your idea of happiness lies in building a business of your own or spending your time in a faraway land, then so be it. What matters most is that you choose to live your own life according to your own terms.

Chase after What You Want

Identify Your Desires

You need to take a step back and rechannel your focus. If you have been an employee for years now, you will find out that the change is going to have a big impact on your life. Changing your current lifestyle into a completely different one is not a decision that you could make overnight. The lifestyle shift needs a series of planning, preparation, and careful execution, so that you wouldn't find yourself struggling in the mud once you decide to take the plunge.

The first thing you need to do is to find out your inner purpose. That includes knowing what makes you happy, what makes you fulfilled, and what makes you want to add value to the world.

If you have always thought of building your own business empire from scratch, then your purpose is to lead and to achieve. Others find solace in silence and taking the life of poverty. Their main purpose in life is to understand the world.

Find your own voice. It is a surprising fact that most people zip through life, following routines and daily schedules, without knowing the very things they want to do. You can pay attention to your interests, hobbies, and personality traits to arrive at a definite life path that will suit your liking.

Identify What You Are Good At

Many people want to become rock stars, actors, and writers. The problem lies in knowing what you want and finding a skill that is related to your desires. If you want to achieve happiness and success in your life, you have to listen to your inner instincts. Find your strengths, and use them to your advantage.

You have already arrived at a definite purpose. If your desire is to sing and to entertain people, then your skill sets should include a talent in singing and making people laugh. Otherwise, what you want is a hobby. Your needs right now must be applicable to your long-term plans, and that means making a career out of something that drives your passion. That is the main reason why you should capitalize, at least, on something that makes full use of your talents.

Find a Way to Get to Your Dreams

This is the tricky part. Many people have successfully lived with their purposes in mind. These are the ones who made the headlines, published books, and became millionaires doing their thing. These are the people who have made it. However, before all the success, there were stories of failure. It is an inevitable part of life. However, that should not stop you from trying.

Finding the balance between your desires and your strong skills will definitely come as a challenge. You will have to be a resilient individual, one who quickly adapts to changes. In the world of the unconventional lifestyle, every day presents an unpredictable opportunity. You have to find the ones you know will help you advance towards the path you desire.

How do you do this? First, be focused and find areas for growth. Do not allow hesitations to form and develop, just go with the flow and trust in all the possibilities. If you aspire to be a teacher and an opportunity to become a tutor (or a teaching aid) comes, then grab it at once. Soak up every knowledge you'd encounter – or in other words, be open to new ideas.

Second, learn to adapt to change. The unconventional way of living is the least secure path to take. So, expect problems to come. There would be many times when you will not get your way, so just remain patient. Always be calm. Be an optimist, and keep pushing until you get your plans into action.

The Choice of Unconventional Living

Your idea of an unconventional lifestyle may not be as radical as spending the remaining years of your life overseas. You may stay at your home country and still face an itch for something as exciting as change. Even so, you are still bound to face difficulties in the presence of your family, your peers, and the system itself.

Here are some common scenarios, which might help you identify what you want. The life design you will make for yourself may contain one, two, or all of these choices.

1. A Change in Career

Your current job may be earning you plenty of money, but you still cannot ignore the emptiness you are going through. You crave for something new, and you want to shift into a different career (which you think is more suitable to your skills, talents, and interests). Income is one thing, but your happiness is not something you should sacrifice in exchange of a big paycheck.

2. Moving Abroad

Moving to a foreign land with no family and friends is a big decision. It is a challenge that you will face on your own, should you continue your choice. However, going out of your comfort zone will also force you to open your mind to different notions. You will meet new people, hopefully have new friends, and understand the way people live on the opposite part of the continent.

3. Being Your Own Boss

Maybe your purpose lies in being a maker of things. The call of self-employment is an attractive one as you get to handle your own time, be closer to family and friends, watch the world go by, and decide in your own terms. However, expect a bumpy ride ahead. There would be months of struggle, as you start your own firm and as you adjust to being your own employer. In exchange of the risk, you will learn how to be a one-man team and how to manage your time and efforts well.

4. Traveling

Traveling is always an exciting path. You get to see different cultures, and have a deeper understanding of how the world works. This is a better choice to make if you want to explore different countries and visit unexplored territories without having to completely abandon the life you have been born into.

5. Defying Norms and Traditions

There are norms and traditions that do not hold as much value today as they did before. A common example is marriage. Women may now choose to skip marriage, or to delay it to an older age. Gender identity also comes into play, as marriage is no longer for a man and a woman only.

The best decision to make is the one you think would best make you happy. Do not go with tradition if you think it would not be in line with your personal goals and possible lifestyle.

Keep Your Head High

Naysayers will come and go. There is no escape from them, especially not if you are dreaming of living a not-so-ordinary lifestyle. At the end of the day, it is up to you to shape life according to how you see fit. Making a lifestyle plan that is relevant to your beliefs, values, skills, talents, and interests will definitely spell a life of happiness and, eventually, success. Just be sure to go with your decisions and live life with no regrets.

Change and Improve Your Life

Refocus Your Efforts

The life-changing concept was built to force a full-degree turn in one's life. That is why it is not for everyone. This is the reason why it is unconventional. That's also the reason why it is scary and definitely not for the faint of heart.

It is almost akin to throwing your past life away in order to make room for a new one. Imagine yourself spending years in a corporate job while continuously dreaming for a long weekend at the beach. To make every day as if it is a weekend, you'd have to make changes – starting with your job. You need to refocus your efforts to follow the lifestyle you designed for yourself.

You have to start again. The life you once knew as a 9-to-5 employee would be a thing of the past. If this scares you enough, then you know you are aiming for something bigger than you have ever imagined.

A design that goes through the unbeaten path is worthy of note. Not everyone has the courage to make the change, so praise yourself for making a risky decision. The change will be hard at first, but you will like it afterwards. Refocus your efforts into something greater and the universe will reward you for the risk that you took.

Be a Bit Selfish

Following the status quo means you have to always think of others before you act. That is why traditions are made. This view in particular is not bad per se. In fact, it is an altruistic perspective. However, you should also prioritize your needs and wants over those of others, so that you would have a happy life yourself.

When you give and offer every time, you wouldn't learn to love yourself in the long term. You owe to yourself the need to be happy, and you could only do that by listening to your inner desires and making them come true.

It is also impossible to give when you have nothing left. A proper design puts you in the spotlight – going with what you want. If life is a stage, then you are the actor. Be a little selfish by fulfilling your needs first. Once you have become a well-rounded individual, it is now time to give back and help others.

Give Back to the Community

The lifestyle design improves people's lives in a way that individuals who were crazy enough to shake things up also made an impact in the lives of the greater majority. For example, if you have spent so much time listening to your own thoughts, then you will become a matured individual and eventually be a good listener.

You might also notice how those who succeeded in pursuing their passion are the ones who were able to inspire change in different ways. The tech billionaire Bill Gates followed an unconventional lifestyle concept by pursuing his dreams in computer programming. He eventually opened his own multimillion-dollar company, which is now known as the Microsoft Corporation. Currently, he is donating billions to various charitable causes around the world.

If that is not enough proof how a good lifestyle plan is able to help other people, then consider the life and creation of Mark Zuckerberg. He is the brains (and brawn) behind the highly successful social networking site, Facebook. Zuckerberg was able to change modern life by creating a site on which people can easily reach out to others. Because of this invention, it has now become easier to talk to people and stay updated.

Push Your Limits

The only thing to do to become great at something is to take a risk in life. Lifestyle design helps people become creative, innovative, and forward thinking. Since the implementation of the concept results into a complete 360-degree turn (from one kind of life to another), you will be forced to make changes and incorporate new ideas. This will inevitably lead to you discovering your limits – pushing existing boundaries and developing new strengths.

This is just one of the benefits linked in following the unconventional lifestyle. You will also raise your standards for excellence, get to know yourself much more, and become better at what you do. Pushing your limits to the maximum is a great way to invent new things and systems that could potentially add value to the world and to humanity.

Idealists have a separate strength of their own. They believe in the good ideas, the rosy perspectives, and the optimist outlooks. If you condition yourself that there is no limit to what your abilities can achieve, then you become capable of doing so much more than you know you could.

Practice Mindfulness

Following a life-changing notion is all about adopting an idealistic approach to living. In the fast world that many live in now, that is not such a bad thing. Sometimes, all people need is quiet, so they can enjoy their lives better. The trouble with following the rules is that you are restricted in terms of what you could do. The trouble with following schedules is that you are not free to do as you wish.

Months and years could pass by, yet you do not have clear memories as to what happened in between. You are usually just "fast forwarding" and then, eventually, you wake up old and devoid of the time and energy needed to enjoy living.

One of the things that a good design gives is clarity and mindfulness when it comes to the present. Most people nowadays are either stuck in the past or anxious of the future. However, if you decide to go the uncharted route, then you will feel more alive and more appreciative of what you have.

You will get to enjoy time, freedom, and social engagement. More than that, you will have more choices. You will live with purpose, and you'll satisfy your thirst for meaning.

Pay Attention to What Really Matters

The age-old question asks: what is the meaning of life? Is it for fun and pleasure only? The answer's "no". Countless issues in the world need to be solved. Is life for happiness? To a certain extent, since one of the key goals in living is to be happy and to make wonderful memories.

Life is created for a purpose. Each person has a different purpose that's waiting to be discovered firsthand. The life-altering concept can help people become acquainted with their inner desires and turn their purposes into reality. The sooner you'd know what destiny really is, the quicker you'll learn how to control your life and bring change to the world.

To do that, you'd have to pay attention to what really matters – people, causes, ideas, and universal goodness. You only have one life, so make the most of it. Create your own lifestyle design and start taking charge of your own destiny.

24

Conclusion

The rewards given by entrepreneurship are tremendous. Those who want to attain a great level of freedom without fear of risks are the types who are most likely to succeed in this special lifestyle and vocation.

We have enumerated all the skills of a good entrepreneur - Creativity, marketing, leadership, product value and ethical standards. These are the skills that make up a good leader. Without one of these, success of the business is difficult to achieve.

The next step now is for you to change how you view yourself as an entrepreneur. If you think you lack one of the 5 skills, then I recommend that you start cultivating it now. Those 5 skills can be learned. You can enhance and strengthen them so if you lack one of the mentioned skills, don't worry because you will eventually develop it.

I also shared with you some ideas on how to get started as an entrepreneur. These ideas are simple and anyone with a bit of discipline and focus can start making money within a few weeks. It is up to you to make a choice to take action.

Lastly, I shared with you the idea of lifestyle design. Lifestyle design and entrepreneurship is something that goes hand in hand. Combining the two is something that in the modern world is possible. With the internet, we now can design the way we want to live. This is of course only possible with hard work and perseverance.

If you believe that you are ready to start your business and if you are confident that you can be a good entrepreneur, I congratulate you. You may now proceed and contribute in making the world a better place.

Good Luck

Thank You

I want to thank you for reading this book! I sincerely hope that you received value from it!

If you received value from this book, I want to ask you for a favour. Would you be kind enough to leave a review for this book on Amazon?

Ó Copyright 2019 by John Winters - All rights reserved.

This document is geared towards providing exact and reliable information in regards to the topic and issue covered. The publication is sold with the idea that the publisher is not required to render accounting, officially permitted, or otherwise, qualified services. If advice is necessary, legal or professional, a practiced individual in the profession should be ordered.

- From a Declaration of Principles which was accepted and approved equally by a Committee of the American Bar Association and a Committee of Publishers and Associations.

In no way is it legal to reproduce, duplicate, or transmit any part of this document in either electronic means or in printed format. Recording of this publication is strictly prohibited and any storage of this document is not allowed unless with written permission from the publisher. All rights reserved.

The information provided herein is stated to be truthful and consistent, in that any liability, in terms of inattention or otherwise, by any usage or abuse of any policies, processes, or directions contained within is the solitary and utter responsibility of the recipient reader. Under no circumstances will any legal responsibility or blame be held against the publisher for any reparation, damages, or monetary loss due to the information herein, either directly or indirectly.

Respective authors own all copyrights not held by the publisher.

The information herein is offered for informational purposes solely, and is universal as so. The presentation of the information is without contract or any type of guarantee assurance.

The trademarks that are used are without any consent, and the publication of the trademark is without permission or backing by the trademark owner. All trademarks and brands within this book are for clarifying purposes only and are the owned by the owners themselves, not affiliated with this document.

www.ingramcontent.com/pod-product-compliance
Lightning Source LLC
Chambersburg PA
CBHW021811170526
45157CB00007B/2543